AIDS – A MORAL ISSUE

Aids – A Moral Issue

The Ethical, Legal and Social Aspects

Edited by
Brenda Almond
Director of the Social Values Research Centre
University of Hull

St. Martin's Press   New York

First published in the United States of America in 1990

Printed in Hong Kong

ISBN 0–312–04204–3

Library of Congress Cataloging–in–Publication Data
AIDS: a moral issue: the ethical, legal and social aspects/edited
by Brenda Almond.
p. cm.
Some of the articles, which have been rev. for this vol., were
originally presented at a conference.
Includes bibliographical references.
ISBN 0–312–04204–3
1. AIDS (Disease)—Social aspects. 2. AIDS (Disease)—Moral and
ethical aspects. I. Almond, Brenda.
RC607.A26A34523 1990
362.1′969792—dc20   89–29380
                                                           CIP

Royalties from the sale of this book will be donated to charities helping people with AIDS

Contents

Acknowledgements

The editor and publishers wish to thank the following for permission to use material from previously published articles in a form specially revised for this volume.

The *New Law Journal*, for use in Chapter 9 of material which first appeared in an article entitled: 'AIDS: Adapting the Law' by Alistair Orr, vol. 138, 1988.

The *Journal of Medical Ethics*, for use in Chapter 9 of material included in 'Legal AIDS: Implications of AIDS and HIV for British and American Law' by Alistair Orr, vol. 15, 1989, no. 2, and also for permission to reprint Chapter 6, 'Autonomy, Welfare and the Treatment of AIDS' by Roger Crisp, vol. 15, 1989.

The *Times Higher Education Supplement*, for use in Chapters 1 and 12 of material included in 'Tackling AIDS' by Brenda Almond, 4 March 1988.

Ethics and International Affairs, for permission to include in Chapter 1 part of 'AIDS and International Ethics' by Brenda Almond, vol. 2, 1988.

The *Journal of Applied Philosophy*, for permission to reproduce with additions the article 'AIDS and Medical Confidentiality' by Grant Gillett, vol. 4, 1987.

While much of the material for this book has been specially written for it, some of the articles included were originally written for the Surrey conference at which the project was initiated. It is of interest to note, too, that many of the contributors were present on that occasion. Those early articles have all been extensively revised for this volume in the light of subsequent developments, as well as further reflection on the part of their authors.

In conclusion, it must be said that a particular debt of thanks is owed to Henry Rosenberg and John Lord of Surrey University for their early assistance in initiating this project and for their continuing encouragement and advice. The editor also wishes to thank Donald Harris of the Centre for Socio-Legal Studies at Wolfson College, Oxford, for reading and commenting on Chapter 9, and Joost Jöbsis for reading and commenting on Chapter 3. Thanks are also due to Paula Cohen for her help and advice in the preparation of the volume.

BRENDA ALMOND

Notes on the Contributors

Brenda Almond is Director of the Social Values Research Centre at the University of Hull, where she initiated a project on AIDS education. She is Chair of the Society for Applied Philosophy and Joint Editor of the Journal of Applied Philosophy. Her books include *Moral Concerns* and *Philosophy or Sophia: a philosophical odyssey.* She is a member of the Institute of Medical Ethics Working Party on the Ethical Implications of AIDS.

Anthony Coxon is Emeritus Professor of Sociological Research Methods, University of Wales, and Research Professor of the University of Essex. He is a principal investigator of Project SIGMA (the national study of sexual behaviour and HIV seroprevalence among gay men in the United Kingdom), co-ordinator of the gay and bisexual men's studies of the Global Programme on AIDS of the World Health Organisation, and a member of a number of voluntary and statutory organisations concerned with AIDS and HIV infection.

Roger Crisp is Research Fellow at the University of Durham. He was formerly lecturer in Philosophy at St Anne's College, Oxford and has also taught at Magdalen College, Oxford. His publications include articles in applied ethics, concerning euthanasia, vegetarianism and advertising. He is currently preparing a book on moral philosophy.

Grant Gillett is a neurosurgeon and Senior Lecturer in medical ethics at the University of Otago Medical School. He is also a Lecturer in the Department of Philosophy and former Fellow in Philosophy, Magdalen College, Oxford. He has published both in philosophy of mind and in medical ethics in journals such as *Mind, Philosophy, Inquiry, British Journal of the Philosophy of Science, Analysis* and *The Journal of Medical Ethics.*

John Lord is Senior Assistant Librarian at the University of
Surrey. He previously worked as a specialist subject librarian
for Philosophy at the university, and has recently completed a
thesis on the philosophical objections to parapsychology.

Anthony Lovegrove is a chaplain at the University of Surrey.
He studied for the priesthood at St John's, Wonersh. After
ordination he read philosophy at Louvain University, and
returned to St John's where he lectured until 1980.

Julian Meldrum worked from 1979 as a volunteer for the
Campaign for Homosexual Equality and the National Council
for Civil Liberties. From 1981 to 1982 he was engaged in
setting up the Hall-Carpenter Archives, a lesbian and gay
educational charity. In 1983 he was briefly involved in a
steering group which formally established the Terrence
Higgins Trust as the first British voluntary organisation
specifically concerned with AIDS. From 1984 to 1986 he wrote
a weekly column on AIDS as health correspondent of the
London free newspaper, *Capital Gay*. He went on to become
Press, Publications and Publicity Officer for the National
Schizophrenia Fellowship, the nearest British equivalent to the
US National Alliance for the Mentally Ill.

Alistair Orr is presently working towards a doctoral thesis on
consent to medical treatment as a Snell Exhibitioner at Balliol
College, Oxford, and is also conducting research at the Centre
for Socio-Legal Studies, Wolfson College, Oxford. He
graduated from Glasgow University with a Law Degree and a
Diploma in Legal Practice.

Anthony Pinching is Senior Lecturer and Honorary Consultant
in Clinical Immunology at St Mary's Hospital Medical School,
London. He is actively involved in clinical care of people with
AIDS and HIV infection and in clinical and basic research on
HIV and AIDS. He is a member of the Department of
Health's Expert Advisory Group on AIDS and was specialist
adviser to the House of Commons Select Committee's Inquiry
on AIDS (1987). He is also a member of many national and
international advisory bodies on AIDS.

Michael Smithurst is a Lecturer in Philosophy at the University of Southampton, and has previously taught at the Universities of Hull, Oxford, Surrey and the City University of New York. His principal interests are in philosophy of science and the philosophies of Hume and Wittgenstein.

Carole Ulanowsky is a Teacher-Fellow in the Social Values Research Centre at the University of Hull. Her research is concerned with education for personal relationships in the age of AIDS. An antenatal teacher for the National Childbirth Trust, she has published articles on education for parenthood and on sex education.

Patricia Wilkie is Director of Counselling at the London Medical charity WATCH (Women in the Counselling of HIV), which is concerned with women and AIDS. She was formerly a Research Fellow in the Department of Psychology at the University of Stirling and AIDS counsellor in the Haemophilia Unit at Glasgow Royal Infirmary.

Prologue: An AIDS Fable

One day a kind animal-lover heard of the plight of the rabbits at Watership Down who were threatened with the loss of their natural habitat. He was a rich man so he bought a large park and made it completely self-contained with large fences that extended as far down beneath the earth as they reached upwards. Then he invited the rabbits to make their home there free from any external risk. They accepted eagerly and soon there was a thriving community of rabbits.

But it happened that one moonlight night, four or five of the rabbits were frolicking in a clearing in the park when they noticed a lush green plant, quite unlike anything they had seen before. Thoughtlessly, they rushed to devour it, unaware that it had poisonous qualities. The poison, however, was very slow-acting, so that the small group of rabbits continued their life in the park, unaware of the strange infection that had entered their system. But whenever they mated with another rabbit, that rabbit, too, became infected, and so did their offspring and rabbits that subsequently mated with the rabbits *they* had mated with.

After some time, two or three of the frolicking rabbits became ill and died. Then many of the rabbits in the park became ill with the same kind of symptoms, and the rabbits realised that something was seriously amiss. They got in touch with their benefactor, who was very concerned. He sent them a friendly scientist who investigated the mysterious illness and worked out something of the truth of the story. But by then many rabbits were dying, and he explained to them that unless they acted very quickly, Watership Park would soon be devoid of rabbits.

So they called a meeting of all the rabbits. But instead of confronting their problem together, they began to split into factions. Those rabbits who lived nearer the place where the plant had grown reacted angrily to attempts to establish whether this was so or not – ignoring the possibility that knowing where the danger had come from might be some help in understanding it. And though rabbits who got the disease were very sick and very miserable, other rabbits turned on them and abused them. Soon rabbits panicked and began attacking any rabbit they thought might have been anywhere near a sick rabbit. They also looked out for rabbits with the same kind of fur patches as the first rabbits to have been infected, since coincidentally it happened that the original group looked rather alike, and they bit and ill-treated these. Then, since there was no way of curing the disease, and it was very unpleasant to know that you had it, some rabbits insisted that they had a right not to try to find out if they had become infected (even though the friendly scientist had found a way of telling whether a rabbit was infected or not long before it became ill). They also wanted to keep it a secret if they *did* find out they were infected, some because they thought they could be very careful not to infect other rabbits, but others because they did not care what happened to the other rabbits and wanted to go on mating in the same way as before.

There are two alternative endings to this story. In one ending, the rabbits decide to confront their plight with total honesty and courage. Every rabbit is made responsible for checking for infection before mating and they agree to take strong measures against any animal who knowingly puts another at risk. The friendly scientist is allowed to ask all the questions he wants to, and all the rabbits answer truthfully and do not take offence if it turns out that their bit of the park has more sick rabbits than other parts. At the same time all the sick rabbits are cared for and no one is allowed to attack another rabbit or stop it getting access to the lettuce and carrot patch just because it has become infected or just because it has the same sort of fur patches as the ones who first became ill. The situation is explained to baby rabbits, even though their mothers would rather have kept them in ignorance till they were a little older. But all the rabbits recognise that this feeling must take second place to the need to make it possible for young rabbits to get to the mating stage without infection, so that they can bring up *their* litters.

I do not know the end of this version of the story, but I know the friendly scientist was working very hard to find a solution to the problem that would allow the rabbits to return to their old carefree existence in Watership Park.

The second ending is not so happy. As the rabbits argued and fought and held huge councils, without, however, doing very much at all, and as rumour abounded and no one believed anyone else, the rabbits went on mating with each other in the same old way until there were so few uninfected rabbits left and so few healthy rabbits born that the species simply failed to survive and the park returned to its original pre-rabbit calm.

BRENDA ALMOND

1 Introduction: War of the World

Brenda Almond

Twice this century the world has been swept by global war, taking with it a massive toll of young lives. In recent years, the slogan 'Make love, not war' has understandably found favour with many people as a personal reaction to the politics of destruction and aggression which made these events possible. This is particularly so in countries where personal freedom is extended to matters of life-style and sexual behaviour.

It is an irony, then – comparable to the twists of a Greek tragedy – that, without the firing of a shot, the world should now be on the brink of a third catastrophe of at least equivalent proportions. Responsible authorities speak of millions of anticipated deaths from Acquired Immune Deficiency Syndrome (AIDS), and figures bear comparison with estimates of the likely casualties of nuclear war. However, the *proportionate* figures are, possibly of more significance in relation to this disease, and there are towns in some countries of central Africa where local medical and health workers estimate that a quarter of the population may be affected by the virus which causes AIDS, while health authorities in the United States have put the figures for men in the relevant age groups in the cities of New York and Philadelphia at 1 in 15. It is not difficult to forecast that, once the virus that causes AIDS is as extensively distributed in human populations as these figures suggest, control of further spread poses a problem of enormous dimensions.

It is not surprising, therefore, that AIDS should have become, as it has, a major political issue on both a national and an international scale. This has both a good and a bad aspect. It is good because action at a national and an international level is needed to combat the disease; it is bad, however, because politics tends to divide when it is necessary to be united, to produce an adversarial response when what is needed is fellow-feeling and a common sense of human vulnerability. In addition, there is an incipient tendency for the Third World and the wealthier nations to confront each other in a spirit of mutual recrimination and to deny unpalatable facts.

Parallel to this international disharmony there is a tendency *within* countries to identify current transmission with particular groups in a spirit of scapegoating, or to polarise the issue on a left–right axis, with the protection of civil rights being set against the taking of strong measures to control the spread of the virus. It would be absurd, however, and even potentially disastrous, if people generally were to associate attempts to prevent or control the spread of the virus with the political right, and indifference to this issue with the political left. For the right is also concerned with civil liberties; the left is also concerned with survival.

How have these misperceptions come about? In part, at least, as a result of an accidental conjunction of factors. In particular, they have come about because AIDS first burst into public consciousness in the early 1980s as a disease primarily affecting white male homosexuals in the Bay area of San Francisco and, not long afterwards, New York. Later, an understanding of the mode of spread of the virus – that it requires the transmission of bodily fluids: semen, and also blood – added two other categories to what have come to be known as 'high-risk' groups: prostitute women and intravenous drug-users (through the practice of sharing needles). That the disease had already for some time been affecting the general population in large parts of sub-Saharan Africa only gradually reached the consciousness of people outside the medical and scientific professions, but even by these the fact was at first discounted as being attributable to other factors not present in Western Europe or America, such as poor sanitary conditions or shortage of medical supplies. So, notwithstanding this major exception, the disease came to be seen, and still is seen by many people, as an affliction of marginal groups.

People of liberal or 'leftist' leanings then respond by seeing the ethical and legal issues generated as essentially matters of civil liberties: the marginal groups must be protected against the discrimination that is prompted by their assumed connection with a lethal and incurable infectious disease. As for responsibility to guard against the spread of infection, this, they argue, is the concern of everybody else – it is second and third parties who must take precautions, specifically in relation to their sex lives, on a kind of sexual *caveat emptor* principle. At the same time, the right, perceiving the issue in terms of guilt and innocence, of morality and immorality, seeks solutions in legislation directed *against* the target groups: the re-criminalisation of homosexuality, for instance, or compulsory quarantining – the latter a policy they see as likely to affect only these relatively small marginal groups and not themselves as part of the uninvolved majority. They have not considered such cases, for example, as that of a married woman with young children, not herself involved with drugs or extra-marital relationships, whose husband's secret affairs or liaisons may have exposed him, and therefore her, to the virus.

This latter example suggests, however, that, following the phase in which AIDS has been seen as a discrimination issue and, in particular, a homosexual or gay rights issue, it should now be regarded as a feminist issue. For the next stage of the virus is one in which the pattern is increasingly one of men infecting women. This will be a transitory phase, however, for in the end AIDS is *everyone*'s issue. Even complacent mature heterosexuals looking back on twenty or more years of settled marriage will find that the virus affects *their* lives too, in the threat that it poses to their sons and daughters.

All this is to talk about the issue in distinctly individual and personal terms. And this is a remarkable feature of AIDS as social and political phenomenon. For most such issues, particularly those with an international dimension, are beyond the control and influence of the individual, and conversely have little direct and immediate effect on personal life. But AIDS is not like this. The threat is *to* the individual in the deepest and most personal and intimate area of life, and action to guard against that threat can also, to some extent, be taken immediately and directly *by* the individual. At the same time, certain kinds of legislative action, as well as governmental inaction, may have a direct and immediate effect on the personal life of the individual.

But there have been epidemics, even pandemics, before. Why should AIDS be seen as such a special case, a problem with so many dimensions? To understand this, it is necessary to recognise the special features of this disease. The first ground of its uniqueness is that it combines two features not previously found together in quite such stark and absolute terms. These are, firstly, that it is most prominently a sexually transmitted complaint and, secondly, that it is a deadly disease lacking at present any medical means of prevention or cure.

To expand these characteristics a little further, it is necessary to say that, in the case of this disease, a person, once infected, is infected for life – but also infectious; that this condition is without visible effects for a number of years, during which a person becomes increasingly more, not less, infectious to others. 'Infectious', however, is to be understood not in the sense of more modest illnesses, in which a disease may be easily passed from person to person in ordinary social contact, but in the sense that it is likely to be transmitted only in highly specific ways: sexual intercourse or blood to blood contamination.

As far as the absence of a cure is concerned, it is important to stress that this is a virus infection, and that modern advances in medicine have not produced *cures* for virus infections. Medical treatment of the many other virus illnesses to which people are subject consists in alleviating the *symptoms* of the illness until the sufferer's immune system itself overcomes the infection. But the AIDS virus *destroys* the natural immune system, so creating a problem that has never before been encountered. These medical aspects, briefly stated here, are discussed fully in Chapter 2 by Dr Anthony Pinching, who sets the scene for the wider debate by introducing some early perceptions of AIDS and examining key aspects of the human immunodeficiency virus (HIV), its transmission, the determinants of HIV spread and the clinical consequences and natural history of HIV infection. Some special problems facing haemophiliacs are discussed by Patricia Wilkie in Chapter 3.

THE WORLD PROFILE OF AIDS

But if AIDS is a serious problem for the individual, it is also a dramatic problem on a world scale. By the end of May 1989 the total number of cases reported to the World Health

Organisation from 175 countries was 151 790 cases, but this is likely to be considerably short of the actual number of cases because of varying degrees of reliability in reporting and collecting data. In addition, it is estimated that the number of people who are already carrying the virus – are seropositive – lies somewhere between five and ten million. The World Health Organisation predicts that fifty million people, mainly in Africa, will be infected within the next five years. The proportion of those affected by the virus who it is expected will go on to develop AIDS and AIDS-related complex (ARC) has risen from early lower estimates of perhaps 17 per cent to 35 per cent, 40 per cent and beyond. Finally, it is assumed, most chillingly, that all those who become ill will indeed die, not of AIDS itself, but of one of the many illnesses to which they fall victim as their immune system is destroyed.

It is unfortunately possible, however, that all these figures, formidable as they are, will eventually be revised in an upward direction: the estimate of the proportion affected who will become ill; the figures of those who are HIV-positive; and the figures of people actually suffering from AIDS. For, despite the limited and highly specific ways in which the virus is known to be communicated from person to person, sexual transmission alone is sufficient to provide for an exponential spread. Some figures from Belgium illustrate this in relation to the case of a single male engineer who died of AIDS. In the previous seven years, before he had had any reason to believe he was ill – and indeed before anyone could have been conscious of the deadly threat so recently arrived on the scene – he had had sexual relations with seventeen women (as well as two others who could not be traced) of whom no less than ten were subsequently found to be seropositive.[1] Clusters of this nature illustrate the potential for spread of the virus in heterosexual populations in metropolitan areas where health standards are high.

Globally there are two main sites of the disease: sub-Saharan Africa, where it is believed that the disease may have originated, and the United States. In the latter country, which has probably the best statistical records for the disease, 97 193 cases had been identified by May 1989 and the US Centers for Disease Control (CDC) in Atlanta estimate that one and a half million American men have the virus. This amounts to one in thirty American men aged between twenty and fifty.[2]

One other salient characteristic of the disease must be mentioned: this is that, unlike many other diseases, such as cancer, with which mankind has reluctantly learned to live, AIDS involves unacceptably *early* death, so that the CDC estimate that by 1991, it will become the second largest cause of lost years of expected life in America. It may already have reached this point or surpassed it in some parts of Africa.

In considering the global situation it is illuminating, and may be useful in responding to the threat, to see the world as divided into three areas: developed western liberal nations; the countries of Eastern Europe; and Third World nations. The liberal democracies have taken individual freedom in the sexual sphere as part of their ethos and way of life; they have also embraced the principle of freedom of travel for their citizens. In their case, then, sexual liberation, combined with geographical mobility, have provided the conditions for the rapid spread of the virus. The countries of Eastern Europe have on the whole endorsed a sterner personal morality; they have tended to reject what they see as the permissiveness of western society and have not attached value to individual freedom in the sexual sphere, other than in state-approved and regulated ways. Neither have their citizens been free to travel between countries with ease and frequency. These countries, it appears, are at the present time less affected by the disease. Third World countries have borne the brunt of the disease, where the low budgets available for medical care, education and the spread of information about the mode of transmission of the virus have added to the difficulties.

Parts of Africa, however, are recognised as having the most serious AIDS problems in the world. Particularly affected are the regions around the great lakes: Uganda, Burundi, Zaire and Tanzania. In Africa it is generally agreed that the spread of the disease is through heterosexual rather than homosexual activity, and through contaminated blood supplies and medical equipment. Frequently the disease there is encountered as a concurrent infection with other diseases. The problem in Africa is compounded by the inadequacy of the resources available to cope with the scale of current AIDS cases: health expenditure may amount to no more than $4–$5 per person per annum, while the cost of screening a single donation of blood would be $4. Syringes *have* to be used more than once and cannot be properly sterilised.

In the light of these economic and practical limitations, statistics from parts of the African continent are daunting. In towns of some affected countries a quarter of the population of child-bearing age are estimated as being affected by the virus, and AIDS accounts for a quarter of the deaths in one leading Kinshasa hospital. At the same time, 10 per cent of the blood stored is believed to be infected.

NATIONAL POLICIES AND INITIATIVES

Action taken by governments in the light of their problems, or of their perception of their problems, varies. In some countries the reporting of AIDS is mandatory, as is sometimes, too, the reporting of positive test results. Others have decided to opt for voluntary systems. The United States early adopted screening for the military and for the Foreign Service, and in June 1987, President Reagan announced an intention to screen migrants, prisoners and applicants for marriage licences. Two days after his announcement a bill requiring mandatory screening of immigrants was passed by the Senate of the United States. However, a number of American states have taken or are considering further measures, some seeking the right to detain infected persons who do not take steps to avoid spreading the disease: the so-called 'recalcitrant cases'. Such legislation usually places the burden of proof on the state to show that the individual is endangering other human beings, and also tends to contain strict confidentiality provisions, with fines or imprisonment as penalties for public disclosure of the results of an AIDS test.

A number of countries have limited policies of screening foreign students, workers and business visitors. India, China and Russia have been reported as adopting this stance. Russia acknowledges that it has deported at least thirty people with AIDS, and India has ordered its five thousand or more African students to be tested or to leave the country. Belgium, too, has decided to insist on tests for students from the Third World who receive grants for their education. Eligibility will depend on a negative test result.

Other areas in which relevant legislative change has been initiated include access to and advertising of condoms – previously normally described as contraceptives, but now increasingly viewed in their prophylactic capacity – a change of emphasis that provides a sufficient reason for this change of terminology. France and Belgium have both passed legislation to liberalise access to condoms, while a number of countries which had legislated against the advertising of condoms on grounds of taste, or because of some people's religious objections, have reconsidered this policy. This includes the United Kingdom, which now permits condom advertisements on television.

THE MORAL PARAMETERS OF LEGISLATION

There is, then, a growing body of law on AIDS and it is clear that governments are likely to be under increasing pressure to act against the threat of the disease. It is important, therefore, to consider not only what laws might be effective but also what are the ethical constraints within which such legislation must operate. The debate on this issue is, as was stated earlier, frequently presented in terms of a conflict between public health and civil liberties, a classic instance of utility (for many) versus liberty (for the few).

On the one hand, there is for the affected individual the possibility of discrimination – of loss of employment or of residence; a risk of public shunning; a possibility of psychological distress acute enough to lead to suicide. And all this in a situation in which a person poses a little or no threat to others in relation to ordinary social living and may personally remain in good health for many years. On the other hand, there is a fear of the spread of a virus so far invulnerable to medical control, and certain to remain so for a number of years ahead, despite the unprecedented speed and urgency of research into possible cures or vaccines.

The legal implications are discussed by Alistair Orr in Chapter 9. He argues that, in its approach to AIDS and HIV infection, the law has to protect two conflicting interests: the right of the public to be protected against the disease, and the right of the individual not to be unfairly restricted as a result of having the disease or of being considered to be at risk. Consequently, he argues, the law must make some compromise which, while protecting public health, will also protect individuals so that they will feel free to come forward for available treatment. This is the way, he suggests, to prevent spread of the disease, and he goes on to discuss how this compromise is or might be affected by British and American law in several areas, including medico-legal matters, criminal and tort law, employment, insurance and education.

The social dimensions are further explored by Julian Meldrum in Chapter 7. In particular, he discusses the way that the issue of AIDS has been treated in the press, and cites examples of cases where individuals have been discriminated against as a result of prejudice and misunderstanding in a context that should call for a maximum of concern and sympathetic understanding. Michael Smithurst, in Chapter 8, argues a strong moral case against discrimination as a response to infinitesimal or non-existent risk. He points out that AIDS is not the only, nor yet the principal, sexually transmitted disease with mortal consequences and he draws a comparison with public attitudes to cervical cancer. He sees the false perception of AIDS as particularly homosexually-related as a main factor in this difference of response.

Smithurst argues that control of sexually-transmitted disease requires willing co-operation and that prejudice against HIV sufferers is counter-productive. He believes that British law in relation to homosexuality is an obstacle to the control of the spread of the disease. Discriminating law and hostile public opinion, he argues, produce secrecy and isolation, hinder dispersal of correct information on HIV infection, and actively prevent extended monogamous relationships in the case of homosexuals.

In discussing the discrimination issue, it is important to separate different aspects of discrimination: against high-risk groups; against people diagnosed as seropositive; and against people with AIDS. The first of these should be, as Smithurst argues, both rationally and ethically a non-issue. *Everyone* is at risk, and every sexually active person is a potential source of infection. So discrimination against particular groups, such as homosexuals, is a response to a phase of the virus which has already passed. In the San Francisco area new cases amongst homosexuals have dropped dramatically; homosexuals have responded to the threat by taking precautions, something they are well able – practically and emotionally – to do.

Heterosexuals, particularly those aiming to have children, have a more difficult problem. This is a subject treated specifically by Carole Ulanowsky and Brenda Almond in Chapter 4, where the problems posed by the threat of HIV infection for women contemplating or embarking on pregnancy are discussed, and some of the impact of the disease on maternity care is assessed. At this juncture, it is sufficient to say, then, that singling out particular groups in the population for discriminatory treatment is a pointless response. It is not even necessary to go beyond this to argue the high moral ground of human rights and civil liberties. Insurance companies, too, are likely to find that discriminating against homosexuals, or even, as has happened in some cases, males living alone, is a policy of diminishing returns if the real object is to save the general insurance subscriber from shouldering the AIDS risk.

But the term 'discrimination' has also been applied to laws and policies relating to persons diagnosed as HIV-positive. It is also much bandied about in relation to the contentious question of establishing whether or not someone is in this category: the issue of testing. It must be said that these are very different issues from the first. The ethical basis for non-discrimination is the ancient principle that equals should be treated equally – that distinctions should be made between people only on grounds which are morally relevant. Now the significant thing about someone who is HIV-positive is that, as a carrier of the AIDS virus, in specific situations, that person may be instrumental in bringing about the illness and death of another person. So if, for instance, within the closed and imposed context of a prison, people are located in different places solely on the grounds that they are HIV-positive or -negative, then this is not a morally irrelevant ground for differentiation. It must be said, however, that it is not a relevant ground for offering less exercise or worse facilities.

Within society at large, however, where people may choose their associates, such separation is both impractical and in most cases unnecessary. This means that discrimination in housing or employment against those who are HIV-positive is unjustifiable. However it is reasonable to argue that a duty to warn sexual partners might be imposed on persons in this position, without this justifying charges of discrimination of unfair treatment.

Finally there is the question of discrimination against people suffering from AIDS. As in the case of the previous group, their protection from arbitrary shunning in work or housing is a right and legitimate cause for campaigning by organisations interested in the preservation of civil liberties, for it is a consequence of the ethical principle that rules out discrimination on non-arbitrary grounds. The limited modes of transmission of the virus make attempts to curtail social contact in these ways an irrelevant and unjustifiable basis for discrimination.[3]

TESTING

The issue of testing is fraught with contention. Many of the contributors to this volume engage with it from various perspectives. Anthony Pinching discusses it from the clinical perspective; Roger Crisp from the viewpoint of various ethical dilemmas in the family doctor's surgery; Alistair Orr from a legal point of view; while Tony Coxon describes the considerations and reactions of gay men before and after taking the HIV test.

Some of the arguments surrounding the issue are practical rather than moral. First, it may be argued that tests need to be offered repeatedly if they are to be effective, since a person may be found negative but shortly afterwards become infected. This argument scarcely merits consideration, since clearly no form of testing could be predictive. Nevertheless it may be useful to establish what *can* be established: that at a particular time and a particular date a person was free of infection. This carries the further useful information that that person's sexual contacts or partners have not been exposed to risk.

This argument may well be based on a slightly different consideration, however. This is that the most widely-used and inexpensive tests – antibody tests – involve a built-in time-lag: 'built-in' in the sense that a person can only be established to be negative by two tests taken at an interval of three months, since the presence of the virus might take this length of time to become detectable. But the development of new forms of testing that make it possible to establish within days whether a person is infectious or not is likely to diminish the force of this particular objection.[4]

Thirdly, however, it may be pointed out that it is statistically likely that testing will involve the misleading discovery of false positives and false negatives, and it must be admitted that false positive results involve unnecessary distress for an individual, and that false negative results may cause an unjustified sense of security leading to risks for others. But, in spite of this, it has to be said that, as tests improve, the incidence of false test results is diminishing, and the usefulness of the vast body of accurate information acquired could well justify toleration of a small amount of error. In any case, repeat testing will in general rule out the possibility that false positive test results will be left to stand, so that this particular problem may be confined to that of a small number of false negative results. Calculations in Canada, for example, which has an extensive testing pro-gramme with wide public acceptance, are that only one result in 50 000 on the ELISA test is a false positive, and when a Western blot test is added the possibility of error is indeed negligible.

Not all the arguments about testing are practical ones. Indeed, it is equally common for ethical considerations to be invoked. In order to consider the issue from an ethical point of view, it is worth setting out the various functions testing may fulfil:

(a) Testing can tell the person tested whether he or she is carrying the virus or not. This itself may be useful to the individual in two ways: first, it informs the individual of whether or not to expect the onset of a serious illness; and secondly it tells the person whether or not he or she is likely to transmit a lethal virus to another person by intimate contact.

Those who oppose testing tend to ignore this second extremely important function. As regards the first, they speak of a 'right to ignorance'. It is true that the news that one is suffering from something that may lead to fatal illness is bound to be unwelcome. Nevertheless there would seem to be a strong moral case for saying that the second function of this knowledge should override the right a person might otherwise be considered to have to maintain peace of mind through ignorance.

Alongside the right to ignorance a 'right to know' is sometimes mentioned as well. This right becomes relevant in relation to proposals for testing the blood supply, or for conducting anonymous surveys designed simply to establish the extent of the spread of the virus in the population. These further functions of testing merit separate discussion:

(b) Testing can enable a medical professional to treat a person whose condition might otherwise be misunderstood; it can enable that medical professional to take appropriate measures to guard against infection in operating on or otherwise treating the person; and it can enable the medical professional to discover whether others are involved who might be at risk, in particular the spouse of a patient, and to consider whether they are adequately protected. This leads to the third function of testing:

(c) Testing is an instrument for guarding the public health. Only if it is known that a person is a carrier of the virus can it be known also whether that person's sexual contacts are at risk, and hence liable to put others at risk. This is not a negligible function, and contact-tracing, with the free co-operation of the person concerned, has long been accepted as a right and responsible strategy in relation to other less serious sexually-transmitted diseases. In addition, testing facilitates public health objectives in a more general way than this, by providing information not otherwise obtainable on the spread of the virus in the population, and on the groups amongst which it is most prevalent.

The strategies suggested by these various functions of testing are sometimes discounted on the grounds that no cure can be offered a person found to be carrying the virus. However this is to overlook the message of the campaign of prevention currently being adopted by many governments. An individual can assume responsibility for ensuring the safety of third parties, in some cases by avoiding the risk altogether, or at

least by taking special precautions (the use of condoms).
Where a person is prepared to take such a responsible attitude,
the intervention of the state would be redundant.

Here the legislation introduced in Sweden in 1985 as an
amendment to its Infectious Diseases Act is of some interest.
This legislation classifies HIV infection as a venereal disease.
In consequence, an obligation is placed on anyone who has
reason to believe that he or she has been infected with the virus
to contact a doctor, who must provide a test in confidential
conditions, and inform the authorities by coded number,
though not by name, if the result is positive. An infected
person is obliged to take measures to prevent the risk of
spreading the disease, and to inform health and hospital
personnel of the risk. In Sweden these measures are seen as
consistent with maintaining the confidentiality of the patient,
and a coded system for laboratory tests and special registration
forms for AIDS patients have been introduced.

Thus it is hard to justify a right to remain ignorant, unless
indeed the desire to remain ignorant is combined with a
willingness to behave as if one had been tested and the result
was positive. (And it is not inconceivable that some people
might prefer this to knowledge.) However one should beware
of using this as an argument for inaction, or as a facile solution
to the problem, as it is used, for example, in a recent
contribution to the discussion by Mark A. Rothstein, who
expresses a very commonly held view when he writes, 'The
same medical advice – in particular, avoidance of high-risk
activities – should be given to both seropositive and seronegative individuals.'[5] This is a statement which takes for granted a
variety of psychological and practical assumptions, some of
them investigated in the study described by Tony Coxon in
Chapter 10. Coxon comments that the assumption that people
will adopt safer sex practices anyway is 'more a pious hope that
a reality'. He reports varying reactions to the test result, but
finds that in general the only event likely to precipitate a major
change of life-style is the death from AIDS of a lover or close
friend.

But Coxon's main concern here is not so much the issue of
testing, but rather how people cope with the threat of
imminent death and take control of their remaining life. He
argues that this important issue is inadequately understood in

the context of AIDS and HIV infection, where the communities most at risk are ill-understood and poorly researched. In
much recent social science research, he suggests, it is
acceptance of one's sexual identity which appears to play a
crucial role in relation to psychological health and longer
physical survival. Coxon examines the implications of this with
respect to gay people, and also considers the issues of
euthanasia and suicide in this context. These are issues touched
on again in Chapter 12.

One further aspect of the recommended advice against
'high-risk' activities is highlighted in Chapter 4. This is that it is
advice specially suited to the case of homosexuals. In other
words, to desist from 'high-risk' activities is advice that can
only be given to heterosexual people if the need to maintain
the processes of conception and child-bearing is ignored. Of
course, not all heterosexual sex is engaged in for this end, but
even here there are problems for securing adherence to 'safer
sex' guidelines. These stem from a double inequality in the
male–female sexual situation: (i) an inequality of power in
decision-making as to whether to take protective measures or
not, and (ii) inequality of risk: the receptive partner is at
greater risk of infection, and females are always receptive
partners in the biological sense.

SCREENING

Where the issue is not individual testing and individual
behaviour, but rather the public policy considerations involved
in anonymous screening programmes, the argument frequently
becomes an argument about the right to know. Here again it is
important to keep the separate functions of testing clearly in
mind, and it would be absurd if public health authorities in
various countries were unable to obtain epidemiological
information without at the same time pursuing the personal
and pastoral aims that are alternative objectives of testing. Few
people know of all the complaints which laboratory examination of their blood might reveal, and the doctrine of informed
consent has not normally been extended to such matters.
Indeed it could be argued that informed consent is essentially
only necessary for treatment, and that a sample of blood that

has been donated for whatever purpose is not a person being treated, but an object being scrutinised.

Common sense, then, suggests some liberalisation of controls in relation to testing. Some would say that it should be possible for medical personnel, including dentists, to ask for a test report before embarking on treatment which may carry additional hazards for them. Some would say, too, that it makes sense to offer HIV testing as routine when treating any kind of sexually-transmitted complaint, unless a patient specifically requests that this should not be done. (This power of veto is needed to ensure that people do not forgo essential treatment through reluctance to be tested.) Such extensions of testing could remove the principal objection to it, in that being tested would no longer be itself a suspect matter, and therefore not an appropriate subject of enquiry by insurance companies or employers.

Ethical considerations, therefore, do not rule out a more positive approach to testing, subject to safeguards for the individual. In addition, through the principle of care for others, they suggest that voluntary testing should be made available as cheaply and conveniently as possible, and in conditions of maximum confidentiality. The same principle, interpreted as a duty of public bodies rather than of private individuals, justifies extensions of anonymous testing, better described as screening, to provide vital epidemiological data independently of medical or personal objectives. This will not, in general, involve referring results back to the person who has provided the blood.

Blood which has been donated for medical purposes such as transfusions raises other considerations. Most countries now accept the need to test blood which is being donated to blood banks and will be used for transfusions to third parties. But should this screening be done in a way which makes it possible to trace the donor of infected blood? Where it *is* possible to do so, would-be donors may be informed in advance, as they are in the United Kingdom, that their blood will be tested and that they will be told of a positive result. This gives them the opportunity to withdraw, and so avoid placing themselves in the situation of taking a test without due consideration. It is an arrangement which removes any possible ethical dilemma from the shoulders of those collecting the blood as to whether to inform or not: in this case, they *will* inform. The overwhelming moral priority here, however, must be the protection of those who may receive donated blood.

There are compelling reasons for saying, too, that blood which is collected for other purposes, and indeed blood collected for research and survey purposes, should be freed from restrictions argued for on so-called ethical grounds, that is, because it may be impossible to give test results to those found positive. The ethical arguments surrounding this issue are discussed in Chapter 5 by Grant Gillett, who concludes that ethical considerations do not prevent the testing of anonymised samples of blood. The priority is to control the spread of the virus, and for this statistical estimates need to be replaced as far as possible by properly researched factual data.

It is only in the light of such information that demands for massive increases in testing programmes can properly be assessed. Clearly this would not be justified for a problem on a modest scale confined to fringe groups. But it is vital, to know whether that *does* accurately describe the nature of the problem, for the time-lag between infection and disease, which may be a matter of years, will make genuinely last-resort measures ineffective.

It is because they have failed to take account of this point adequately that many of the arguments advanced by people concerned about the ethical and legal aspects of AIDS have been arguments for *in*action. Some who have argued against legislative change, however, have done so for a different reason. They have argued that in most countries the law as it stands is already adequate to cover the risks to second and third parties that are implicit in this disease. In particular, for someone who knows he or she is infected to have unprotected intercourse, or to share a needle with another, could amount to murder in the accepted definition of 'reckless indifference to human life' if infection results. Against this consideration, however, it is necessary to weigh the fact that it is unlikely that cause and effect could be effectively demonstrated in such circumstances: again we are in the presence of the lethal time-lag which makes AIDS the problem for the world that it in fact is. So this argument for inactivity, while it may suggest the possibility of interesting legal cases or potential compensation suits, cannot be accepted as an argument against placing stronger duties on individuals both to seek testing and to avoid risks to others.

However the argument may well be effective in relation to ethical arguments concerning confidentiality. For medical professionals, the context may be more like that of criminal dangerousness in cases involving psychological illness, such as the Tarasoff case, discussed by Alistair Orr in Chapter 9.[6] The principle that was appealed to in that case was that necessity trumps other obligations, in particular the obligation of medical confidentiality. So a professional might be seen as having a duty of full and frank disclosure of his or her danger to the spouse of a person infected with the AIDS virus. This subject is discussed in detail by Grant Gillett in Chapter 5, and again in relation to a variety of situations by Roger Crisp in Chapter 6.

Commenting on the way in which many AIDS-related issues are polarised, Crisp points out that, at the social level, civil rights or liberties are seen as being in conflict with general utility, and that an analogous distinction is often assumed to exist at the one-to-one, individual level at which doctors work. Crisp argues that the latter form of the distinction is false. By seeing autonomy as part of welfare, he suggests, doctors can think more directly about such issues as paternalism, confidentiality and consent. He discusses a number of these issues in the light of this revised conception of welfare, in the form of simplified case studies.

A different kind of argument against legal intervention is sometimes based on the claim that agreement to an unprotected sexual act in itself involves acceptance of the risk of AIDS; since what is at issue is acts between consenting adults, it is argued that no obligations and no sanctions need be imposed on the infected person who fails to warn a sexual partner. However, while everyone would be wise to take precautions, it can hardly be maintained that the risk of AIDS must be considered a normal element in a sexual encounter. And one person's knowledge deliberately concealed from the other significantly removes any equality of ignorance, and consequential equality of risk, that might otherwise be claimed.

These are considerations pointing to the justice of introducing new specific legislation on some of the matters under discussion. There are, nevertheless, areas where the intervention of the law may indeed be counter-productive. In particular, the effect of existing criminal law in relation to prostitution, homosexuality and drugs may be to promote unsafe practices in these areas. It may well be that, for instance, the decriminalisation of prostitution in countries where it must operate outside the law will be a necessary further step in the control of AIDS, as may be the apparent condoning of drug use involved in the distribution of free needles.

Finally, is law to be seen operating in this area, as it is sometimes criticised for doing in other areas of law and criminality, as protecting the wealthy and strong against the poor and weak? Those who claim this are likely to claim that internationally, too, coercive policies may be directed at protecting rich and powerful nations against poorer and less influential nations in the Third World. In considering these charges it must be conceded that some factors associated with the spread of AIDS, such as drug use and prostitution, to some extent do characterise the less affluent subcultures of societies. Nor is it surprising that it is amongst such subcultures that AIDS first manifested itself. For in most matters that involve a threat to health, the poor are bound to be susceptible. However the moral to be drawn from this is that these vulnerable groups need the *protection* of soundly constructed legal and social policies; it is not a question of policing vulnerable groups as if they were criminals, but of protecting them as being potentially most likely to be affected.

As for the protection or policing of whole nations, the question remains as to whether it makes sense for some countries to try to keep out by immigration controls people who are affected with the virus. Certainly, wherever this is proposed, it is bound to be a politically popular move, for those affected have no constituency, and those who *have* a constituency – a vote – see themselves as being offered protection. But this is a virus that knows no boundaries, and once it is rife *within* a population, external protection becomes a somewhat pointless curb on freedom of movement. It is an irony, too, that such measures are often most vociferously proposed in countries which are themselves amongst those most affected by the presence of AIDS, such as the United

States. One significant fact to consider here is that the more permissive or sexually liberated a society, the greater the toll that this disease will exact. And it is undoubtedly the case that the United States, Australia and the countries of Western Europe have moved much further in this direction than the countries of Eastern Europe. Therefore Russia's recent decision to test visitors and students is rational if it is true, as claimed, that three-quarters of its small number of AIDS cases have been visitors. It is a sombre thought that the Iron Curtain which has for decades and until very recently controlled freedom of movement between East and West may prove a *cordon sanitaire* against the AIDS virus. In the end, then, the health testing of immigrants remains the prerogative of sovereign nations, and each will in the end form its own judgement as to whether the AIDS threat is greater from without than within.

It should be said that the contributors to this volume write as individuals, expressing their own personal views, and are as varied in their life-styles and personal circumstances as any cross-section of society. What drew them together was an early concern for the ethical and social aspects of AIDS which resulted in a small conference at the University of Surrey in 1986. Most of the contributors would, however, agree on two things: the need to care for others by preserving their life and health; and the need to protect the rights of individuals to self-fulfilment in the area of sexuality. These considerations jointly suggest two parameters for measures to combat AIDS: (i) that these should positively address the need to protect public health; (ii) that they should guarantee strong action to protect individuals against discriminatory treatment or any form of persecution or ill-treatment. In pursuing these aims, it might also turn out to be necessary to free from legislative control aspects of life which it has in the past seemed immoral for society to recognise, in order to bring them within the orbit of health promotion measures.

This two-pronged approach may be contrasted with the one-sided and divisive proposals of those who set civil rights in opposition to public health, and vice versa. Individuals can only be expected to co-operate in necessary public health measures if they can be assured that the law will protect them in their personal lives from intimidation and discrimination, enabling those who are affected by a long-term episodic illness, for example, to continue, as long as they are able, to earn a living and maintain residence in their own community.

In the following chapters various facets of these moral requirements will be explored from the medical perspective, the community perspective, and the personal perspective. In Chapter 11, Anthony Lovegrove argues the inappropriateness, from a theological point of view, of a certain sort of moral censoriousness, and in Chapter 12 some tentative conclusions are suggested as to what commitment to certain basic moral principles might mean in practice, both for the individual and for public policy. Finally, the reader is offered a guide, compiled by John Lord, to the growing literature on the ethical, legal and social aspects of AIDS.

Notes

1. N. Clumeck, P. Hermans, H. Taelman, D. Roth, G. Zissis, S. de Wit (St. Pierre University Hospital, Brussels, and Institute of Tropical Medicine, Antwerp, Belgium) 'Cluster of heterosexual Transmission of HIV in Brussels', poster and oral presentation to IIIrd International Conference on AIDS, Washington DC, June 1987.
2. Figures from the Centers for Disease Control, Washington DC.
3. The question of insurance companies' policies in these cases is, however, more complicated. See Mark Scherzer, 'Insurance', in H. L. Dalton (ed.) (1987) pp. 185–200. The two issues of life insurance and medical insurance must be separated. Having a life-threatening medical condition is clearly relevant to the former. As far as the latter is concerned, it is obvious that, one way or another, the community is *bound* to meet medical needs, since no individual's resources are likely to be adequate for this condition.
4. Report on tests developed by Abbott and Du Pont, *New Scientist*, 11 June 1987. These are antigen tests which detect infection faster and also help predict the course of subsequent disease. Quick five-minute tests are also being developed by Cambridge BioScience of Worcester, Mass., USA.
5. Mark A. Rothstein 'Screening Workers for AIDS', in H. L. Dalton (1987) pp. 141ff.
6. See Chapter 9, note 67.

Part I

The Medical Perspective

2 AIDS: Clinical and Scientific Background

Anthony Pinching

INTRODUCTION

It is sometimes said that AIDS presents unique problems. I would qualify that: all the problems are familiar; they have come up with other diseases, in other contexts of medicine, its practice and its ethics. What is unique about AIDS is the very sharp relief into which the issues are thrown by this disease. So it is unique only in the sense that a single disease raises so many difficult issues.

AIDS is relevant to everyone. Yet, especially in the early years of the epidemic, but even now, we find the attitude that it is somebody else's problem. This is applied to its likely impact and to responsibility for taking action, whether in prevention or care. This has been a part of the phenomenon of denial which is perhaps an instinctive human first response to something unpleasant. The next phase for some has been casting blame, another apparently human instinct when unpleasant reality is no longer deniable. Fortunately, increasing numbers of people have moved beyond this to take action, whether in their personal lives or in their professional roles. Those who continue to deny, or who blame others, are rendered incapable of acting on their own behalf of that of their communities.

Within the medical profession denial or blaming may take unusual forms. This may consist of setting limits, for example by excluding from care patients with HIV or AIDS, as if it were a matter of choice, or denying responsibility for the wider repercussions of illness and the medical response to it, as in the issue of HIV testing. I do not find this an acceptable attitude within a caring profession in any moral sense. Working with AIDS has reinforced awareness of the arbitrary nature of such divisions; the problems are ours to share as members of a community. But this emphasises again the need for the community itself to participate, in partnership. AIDS is a new problem, presenting new versions of old challenges, and it is not going to go away during our lifetime.

However, in order to cope with this problem, conceptually or in society, it is vital to understand a few basic facts about the virus, HIV, its transmission, and the range of disease that it causes. Many current perceptions about AIDS have arisen from misunderstandings of the facts – misunderstandings that have in part resulted from distortions in the media and from careless use of words. This brief account is intended to serve as a background for the discussion that follows.

WORDS AND PERCEPTIONS

In early headlines AIDS was referred to as a 'plague'. The word 'plague' refers to bubonic or pneumonic plague. Two discrete aspects of plague as an infectious disease are implied by the term: one is that it is contagious, being very easily passed from person to person in a casual setting. If one person in a room had pneumonic plague, many others present would catch it. Secondly, 'plague' also has the connotation of a nasty disease: it kills. So the use of the word implicitly conveys two separate notions. Only one of these is applicable to HIV and AIDS. AIDS is a very unpleasant and typically fatal disease resulting from HIV infection, but HIV is not contagious like plague or other 'plagues' such as smallpox; it is only transmitted in specific settings of human contact, typically settings of implicit or explicit consent. A person with HIV or AIDS sitting in a room with others will not transmit HIV to others.

THE BASIC STRUCTURE AND PROPERTIES OF HIV

To understand the way in which HIV is transmitted and how it causes disease we must first examine something of its structural attributes and functional properties. HIV consists of two main elements, an outer membrane or envelope, and an inner core. The outer membrane is taken from the cells of the person it infects. This outer membrane determines the physical properties of the virus, in turn determining how it is transmitted and how it is inactivated. The basic constituent of the membrane is fatty material. Since it is not a virus product, it cannot be repaired by the virus.

The lipid membrane of HIV is extremely fragile, being readily disrupted by a variety of environmental influences. Since the virus cannot repair its membrane, disruption leads to inactivation. As a result the virus survives extremely poorly outside the body. In addition, although HIV is in body fluids and secretions of an infected person, including blood, semen and female genital secretions, this is in only small quantities. It is very easily inactivated by a variety of things, including heat, drying, detergents and most standard disinfectants.

In the middle of the virus particle is its nucleic acid, containing its genetic code, and the proteins, whose formation is instructed by the genes. These confer the biological properties, three of which are important. The first is the property of latency, which means that once the virus has infected a cell or, in effect, a person, it persists. So once a person is infected, they are infected for life. This property of HIV results from particular characteristics of its genetic material. The virus gene consists of ribonucleic acids (RNA), but through a virus enzyme known as reverse transcriptase, this can be copied into deoxyribonucleic acids (DNA); this copy can then be spliced into the DNA genetic code of human cells. In this way the virus genetic code is incorporated into the cells of the body that it infects.

Secondly, the infection caused by the virus is a productive infection, in which new virus particles are being produced for all or most of the duration of infection. This means that a person is infectious for life, by the three established routes outlined below, whether they are well or ill. Recent evidence suggests that infectiousness may be greater as a person becomes unwell and also in the weeks after becoming infected, before an immune response develops. However clinical and epidemiological observations indicate that they may be infectious to some degree at any stage of infection.

The third key biological property of HIV is its specific attack on certain cells of the body, the T 'helper' cells and macrophages of the immune system; this leads to its capacity to cause disease. Disease broadly speaking is of two types: progressive immune deficiency, as seen in the AIDS-related complex (ARC) and AIDS itself, due mainly to the loss of T helper cells and their functions, in which a person becomes susceptible to certain infections and tumours; and progressive damage to the nervous system, leading to dementia or loss of motor or sensory function, due to direct or indirect effects of HIV infection in nervous system macrophages.

Most of these key features of the virus were apparent before the type and specific identity of the virus were known. We knew about it in much the same way as we know about the wind, without ever seeing it. We know what it is and how it behaves by virtue of the things that it does.

HIV TRANSMISSION

As a result of its physical properties, HIV is transmitted only in settings of very close and direct human contact. However it is important to appreciate that the routes of transmission have been proved by documenting spread in individual cases and through the study of populations through epidemiology. The patterns of spread that have been established by observing what actually happens are readily understood through a knowledge of virus structure.

HIV is only transmitted by three basic means: (i) most commonly, sexual transmission through penetrative inter-course; (ii) transmission by blood, either by transfusion of blood or blood products from HIV-infected people or, increasingly commonly, by injecting drugs using needles and syringes shared with HIV-infected people; (iii) transmission from an infected mother to her unborn child across the placenta and possibly through breast milk. All instances of HIV transmission that have occurred worldwide to date are explicable in terms of these basic routes, which were established in 1982, within a year of the first reports of AIDS. Casual transmission has not been demonstrated, despite observations on very large numbers of HIV-infected persons living in family or social settings with close casual contact and on those providing care for HIV-infected persons in hospital and in the community.

As regards sexual transmission, there has been a remarkably persistent focus on homosexual transmission, which was the first to become apparent. However, since then it has become clear that HIV is simply a sexually transmissible infection and is spread equally effectively by heterosexual contact, passing from male to female and from female to male. Indeed, worldwide, this route is by far the most common means of transmission. Despite extensive and almost voyeuristic speculation on the mechanics of sexual intercourse, the key issue is penetrative sexual intercourse. Risk is related to numbers of partners and their risk of infection and is not directly related to sex or sexuality. Yet the role of homosexuality itself as a risk factor has been exaggerated beyond reason, revealing pre-existing prejudices and intolerance which had previously been covered by but a thin veneer.

DETERMINANTS OF SPREAD

The main determinants of the rate of spread of HIV and of the groups or individuals at risk are the numbers of sexual partners and their risk of infection. This can be conceptualised with reference to a simple model of a newly introduced, persistently infectious, sexually transmissible virus, spreading in defined populations over time. Spread can initially be viewed in two populations, representing extremes of sexual behaviour. In the first population, most people have only one contact and very few have multiple contacts. In this population, the virus will spread very slowly if at all and, even over long periods, only a small proportion of the population will have become infected. On the other hand, in a population where most people have multiple contacts, the virus will spread very rapidly. Quite soon it will become so common that even those with relatively quiet life-styles will increasingly be at risk. Between these two extremes obviously, are a range of behaviours which will lead to intermediate rates of spread, relative to prevailing rates of contact.

In reality, populations are not as extreme as these, nor are they as homogeneous. In different parts of the world and different parts of any community, there are populations that vary greatly in prevailing norms of sexual behaviour, for a great variety of social, historical and cultural reasons. Usually there is also a great diversity of subcultures within any community that are not isolated from one another, but where individuals may act as 'bridges' between different subgroups and hence between different levels of risk.

The homosexual population in the United States and Western Europe and the heterosexual population in parts of Africa and the Caribbean have included a relatively high proportion of people with multiple sexual partners. Heterosexuals in Europe and the United States on the other hand have tended to have fewer partners, although multiple contacts are not that uncommon. Hence we have seen different rates of spread of infection in different societies around the world and these have also been affected by the time when the virus appeared in each. However the concurrently running epidemics can lead to contacts between groups at lower and higher risk. Thus individual risk is a function not only of what subpopulation they belong to but which one their partner is from, or has had contact with, and so on.

CONSEQUENCES OF HIV INFECTION

There are a number of possible outcomes following exposure to HIV by one of the above routes. Some people may be exposed and do not become infected, as is the case for many other infectious organisms. For example, among regular sexual partners, 40–50 per cent are repeatedly exposed and yet remain uninfected. It is currently estimated that 30–40 per cent of children born to HIV-infected mothers become infected. Differing susceptibility to HIV infection appears to be relative, being affected by virus inoculum and route of exposure, and could be determined by genetic or environmental co-factors.

For those who do become infected, there are a number of possible clinical consequences. However all develop antibodies to HIV within a few months that can reliably identify a person as being infected. HIV antibody testing has therefore been used as a surrogate for the infection itself, since anyone who develops antibodies must have acquired persistent infection, given the nature of HIV. Following infection people are initially asymptomatic for several years and may remain so indefinitely; some have enlarged lymph nodes (persistent generalised lymphadenopathy – PGL). They have HIV infection and are able to transmit it, but show no sign of immune or nervous system damage. It may be that some people who remain asymptomatic for long periods, with or without PGL, have some sort of protective immunity or innate resistance against HIV.

However, in many cases, HIV does cause progressive damage to the immune system or nervous system, leading to symptomatic disease. In the AIDS-related complex there is evidence of moderate immunodeficiency from increased susceptibility to certain minor opportunist infections, together with some constitutional symptoms; such patients are at high risk of progressing to AIDS. In AIDS itself, more severe damage to cell-mediated immunity causes susceptibility to more serious opportunist infections or tumours, that take advantage of the weakened immune defence against them. It is these opportunist events that cause illness in people with AIDS. In HIV encephalopathy, which typically occurs after the development of AIDS but occasionally may precede it, the virus causes progressive damage to the central and peripheral nervous systems, with gradual development of dementia and disorders of sensation and motor control.

NATURAL HISTORY OF HIV INFECTION

We are still defining the long-term consequences of HIV infection from follow-up of people who acquired the infection early in the epidemic. Progression to AIDS has been seen in about 15–20 per cent after 3 years, 30 per cent after 5 years and 50 per cent after 10 years. Although at the longest follow-up some show signs of ARC or other indicators of progression, others remain entirely well. While longer follow-up is likely to show still further rises in attack rate, it remains possible that some will remain well indefinitely. It has also been shown that co-factors may enhance the risk of progression. These include other sexually transmitted infections acquired after HIV, and more than one pregnancy, infants also show more rapid progression. These co-factors may act by activating latent HIV infection. Additional immunosuppressive influences, such as malnutrition, some other infections and immunosuppressive drugs, can also probably increase risk of progression. Most of the numerical estimates of rates of progression are based on people infected early in the epidemic and it is unwise to assume that these groups will necessarily be representative of outcome, since they may be especially susceptible to both infection and disease and may be relatively enriched for co-factors.

ETHICAL ISSUES

These are considered elsewhere in this volume, but it is essential to appreciate that clinicians and others working in prevention, care and research are constantly facing and addressing many of these issues at a very practical and immediate level. The ethical principles underlying analysis of the issues and the decisions resulting are well known, but the resolution must be both pragmatic and far-sighted; implementation in practice requires consistency. In caring for people with a potentially infectious disorder, we have a duty not only towards the patient who seeks care but towards the wider society in which he or she lives, not least for those people who may otherwise become our patients. It is often assumed by those observing from the outside that there is or need be a basic conflict between the need to respect individual rights and those of society in respect of AIDS. I believe this to be a fundamentally flawed assessment. In the vast majority of instances, beneficent respect for a person's autonomy can engender the very responses that are needed for a beneficent respect for the wider social good.

Physicians have a particular advantage in being able to reach affected members of the community. People come forward to seek care on the understanding that the clinician has the primary purpose of offering care without discrimination and will respect and secure confidentiality. In such a setting they will reveal much of their personal background, as it relates to AIDS. This information, otherwise known only to themselves, can serve as the basis for offering advice and education regarding prevention on a one-to-one basis. This in turn offers the means for appropriate behavioural change. The spread of HIV is in essence through private consensual contact. Only through an understanding, by both counsellor and individual, of the nature of such contacts, and relevant advice on behavioural change do we have any chance of influencing spread of HIV. A person's ability to effect such behavioural change will be affected by comprehension and motivation. Tools to assist in the achievement of behavioural change will necessarily be diverse, according to individual personal and contextual attributes.

As an example, for some, the knowledge of an HIV test result, positive or negative, may be helpful in leading to suitable change; for others, it may offer no direct advantage to effecting change, so long as risk is understood, but it may have other adverse personal or social effects; it may even be counter-productive, as for the person who has run high risk in the past but has so far remained negative, who may be thus reinforced in a view that such risk-taking is acceptable. Certainly many proponents of testing seem to imagine some very direct linkage between a test result and a behavioural change, which is at variance with much clinical experience. Indeed the homosexual community, which initially had a very low take-up of testing, has achieved a remarkable slowing of the rate of spread of HIV; this has thus been largely effected through behavioural change adopted regardless of knowledge of personal HIV status.

Testing on a voluntary and confidential basis for those who wish it after pre-counselling and informed consent may be helpful but is only a part of the story. As experience increases and as social attitudes change, take-up of HIV testing is increasing as it is increasingly well-informed and secured. However it must remain a matter for the individual to balance the pros and cons and to adopt behavioural change regardless of the decision taken. Coercion and exhortation are part of the language of discrimination and alienation. They will only serve to isolate the very people whose co-operation we need if we are to affect the course of this epidemic and who need our help. This example should serve as a reminder that respect for a person's autonomy is in fact a vital tool in safeguarding the public health, a viewpoint that echoes repeatedly around all the discussion on ethical implications of AIDS and HIV.

3 Haemophilia, AIDS and HIV: Some Social and Ethical Considerations

Patricia Wilkie

Since the beginning of the AIDS epidemic, those with haemophilia have been recognised as one of the major groups at risk of contracting AIDS. The effect on the haemophilia population of so many of their members having contracted HIV iatrogenically through contaminated blood products has been far-reaching and profound.

Questions of confidentiality and the maintenance of personal privacy, living with uncertainty in the face of life-threatening illness, difficulties in acquiring life assurance, stigma and isolation were all subjects familiar to those with haemophilia and their families before the onset of AIDS. This chapter describes some of the difficulties facing those with haemophilia and how these problems have been exacerbated by AIDS.

AIDS has been described as a lifelong disease which is sexually transmitted. Haemophilia is a lifelong condition which is genetically inherited and therefore genetically transmitted. Throughout the world many haemophiliacs have contracted AIDS through transfusions of contaminated blood. In the United Kingdom 1200 haemophiliacs are known to be HIV-positive out of a total haemophilia population of 5000. People with haemophilia are a clearly identifiable but minority group of those at risk of contracting AIDS, accounting for 1 per cent of those who develop the disease.

Haemophilia, Christmas Disease and Von Willebrands are all disorders of the blood due to a deficiency in the clotting mechanism. The severity of the condition is usually measured by the amount of deficiency of the clotting factor. The effect on a person suffering from one of these conditions is, to a greater or lesser extent, bleeding, often spontaneously, into the joints of the arms and legs. These bleeds can be extremely painful and if left untreated will lead to chronic, crippling deformity of the joints. The treatment of haemophilia has undergone considerable change in the last two decades.[1] Until 1964 the main therapeutic material used in the treatment of haemophilia was fresh frozen plasma in the form of infusions with which the patient was treated in hospital. Since then technological advances in the preparation of Factor VIII and Factor IX, the clotting factors defective in haemophilia, have enabled the preparation of various coagulation factors which can be administered intravenously, either prophylactically or immediately after a bleed. As these preparations can be kept in a domestic refrigerator, programmes of home treatment have developed. Patients are taught to inject themselves intravenously, with the result that the number and severity of bleeds can be reduced, as well as the period of immobility and pain.[2] Furthermore patients need no longer suffer extended periods off school or work. Home treatment has brought a 'normalisation' to the lives of those with severe haemophilia.

By 1983 it was clear that haemophiliacs were at risk of contracting the human immuno-deficiency virus (HIV) that causes AIDS from infusions of contaminated blood products. Factor VIII, which is used in the treatment of Haemophilia A, is produced by a fractionating process out of plasma pools made up of as many as 20 000 individual donations. The pool for the production of Factor IX used in the treatment of Christmas Disease is much smaller, with the result that those suffering from Haemophilia A are more likely to have contracted HIV. In February 1985 the heat treatment of blood products used in the treatment of haemophilia was introduced and in October 1985 the screening of all blood donors for HIV was also initiated. It is hoped that haemophiliacs who have received only heat-treated material will no longer be at risk.

As information about the blood problem became available, haemophiliacs were faced with the difficult task of evaluating the risk of contracting AIDS. For a haemophiliac this risk had to be assessed alongside the risk of contracting another hazard of treatment, hepatitis, and also assessed against the damage to health that would be caused by the reduction in or total cessation of treatment. Patients at Glasgow Royal Infirmary

Haemophilia Reference Centre said that their first reaction to the AIDS crisis was to cut back on treatment. However the general consensus now is well described by one patient: 'There is really no choice. You have to treat yourself. The consequences are too great if you do not. And after all, hepatitis is a greater risk than AIDS.' Nevertheless there has clearly been a dilemma for these patients which is demonstrated by one group of researchers who calculated that the same group of patients who had stated that they continued to treat themselves as usual significantly modified their treatment.[3] It remains to be seen whether this trend continues.

The expectation of life of haemophiliacs is gradually approaching the normal.[4] Nevertheless severe haemophiliacs may still have difficulty in getting life assurance. In fact the present situation is that it may be impossible for people with haemophilia to get life assurance at all without first having their antibody status verified. Existing insurance application forms have questions that can easily elicit the presence of chronic disease and hence haemophilia. It is much more difficult to identify those in other risk groups and not all assurance companies have introduced 'life style' questions in their life insurance application forms. Furthermore it is against the insurance contract knowingly to withhold information that could be relevant to the application, for example that the person has haemophilia, even though the question was not explicitly asked. As haemophiliacs constitute the one very easily identified group at risk of contracting AIDS, it is likely that insurance companies will begin to ask questions explicitly about haemophilia.[5]

Insurance companies have also to consider the possibility that those who have contracted HIV sexually may seek the protection of the Venereal Diseases Act which can protect the individual by prohibiting staff from clinics for sexually transmitted diseases from giving information about antibody status to the patient's own doctor without the consent of the patient. It is arguable that the patient's permission should always be sought before sensitive information is disclosed about him. In the case of haemophilia, however, it is in the best interest of the patient that his own doctor should know of his clinical condition, that is, that the patient has haemophilia.

Prior to the advent of self-therapy and the better control of bleeds, many haemophiliacs tended to hide the nature of their illness. Disclosure could mean no jobs as well as a degree of social isolation. With the improvement in treatment this problem has been less critical for many haemophiliacs who have been able to complete their education and find appropriate employment. However the identification of haemophiliacs as one of the groups at risk of contracting AIDS has changed the situation. In addition there has been considerable publicity in both the national and local press about the problems facing haemophiliac children at school. Their families have not known how to deal with the situation and sometimes school staff and parents of other children have over-reacted. The young haemophiliac is made to suffer loneliness and isolation at a critical time in his life. It is, therefore, not surprising that many haemophiliacs and their families are now reluctant to disclose that there is haemophilia in the family. This may have always been the case with those more mildly affected, who had no visible signs of haemophilia. For the severe haemophiliac, prompt action following a bleed could save his life, so that it may not be in his best interests to hide the fact that he has haemophilia.

Haemophilia is a condition which has an effect on the entire family. Parents, in particular the mother, may have had feelings of guilt about bringing into the world a child with haemophilia. Mothers are very involved in the home therapy treatment and are trained to give the intravenous infusion to their child until he is old enough to do it for himself. Some mothers are particularly concerned that they may have personally administered the infusion or infusions that infected their child with HIV. Unaffected siblings will have experienced the loss of a parent's time and attention. And female siblings may be carriers and will therefore have to explain the inheritance pattern of haemophilia to a future partner. The partners of people with haemophilia are similarly involved and both parents and partners may, from time to time, be involved in giving or assisting with treatment, even if professionally advised against doing so. There is, therefore, some small danger of risk to non-sexual household contacts of HIV-positive haemophiliacs from exposure to contaminated blood or from needlestick injury.

When a young adult haemophiliac is told of his antibody

positivity, he is likely, if resident at home, to tell his parents, who will in turn decide which family members should be informed. Parents do not always know who will be discreet and whom whey can trust to maintain confidentiality. This is a situation that places extreme stress on all the family.

Prior to the appearance of AIDS, haemophiliacs more than most people have had to consider carefully whether they want to have children, as well as having had to discuss with a partner the implications of their own illness and the transmission of haemophilia. Affected males should know that all their daughters will be obligate carriers and their sons unaffected by haemophilia. The partner of an affected male could have pre-natal sexing and selective termination of a female foetus. A female carrier of haemophilia could have prenatal sexing and selective termination of a male foetus, thus preventing the birth of an affected child. It is hoped that the recent discovery of a gene marker will enable more accurate pre-natal diagnosis to be carried out by identifying an affected foetus. These are difficult and, not surprisingly, infrequently used choices for haemophiliacs and carriers. The alternative, however, is to live with the uncertainty and accept the risk of having a carrier daughter or an affected son.

Genetic counselling involves helping people to live with uncertainty. The language of genetics is the language of 'might' and 'may'. It is seldom the language of certainty. Living with uncertainty, and making decisions in the face of uncertainty, presents particular problems for the individuals concerned. Because haemophiliacs attend hospital regularly for treatment, it has been possible to test the antibody status of the majority of those with haemophilia. Those found to be HIV-positive face a long period of uncertainty. While the majority of these patients are still asymptomatic, it must be assumed that a number of these patients will go on to develop AIDS. In genetic counselling there is considerable debate about the appropriateness of early identification of asymptomatic persons at risk of developing a serious disorder for which there is no cure. Undoubtedly, however, even if patients wish to know their antibody status, they will need help to live with the uncertainty of HIV positivity.

The power of positive thought to help stave off the helplessness of passivity is a tactic used by many. Nancy

Wexler in her study of people at risk of developing Huntington's Chorea described how her respondents spoke of staving off the effects of the disease through 'strength of will'. HIV-positive haemophiliacs sometimes express similar views.[6] 'You have got to fight this with the mind: be positive and then you won't get AIDS' is a view expressed by many patients. However a problem with this standpoint is that the individual becomes responsible for the presence or absence of the disease. To develop the disease can then be interpreted as failure of control and can lead to a considerable sense of failure on the part of the person concerned.[7]

Anger is a common emotion when individuals receive unpleasant information. It is not surprising to learn that many haemophiliacs feel very angry about their present situation. To survive they are dependent and will continue to remain dependent on blood products – the products from which they contracted the AIDS virus. Some people with haemophilia see parallels with the thalidomide case. It is frequently stated that it is 'not the fault' or 'not the responsibility' of the haemophiliacs who are HIV-seropositive or who have AIDS and that, therefore, those individuals should be compensated. Some have specifically suggested that there should be compensation for the restrictions imposed by being HIV-positive. In 1987 the British government awarded £10 million for 'recompense' for haemophiliacs who had contracted HIV. The money was awarded to the Haemophilia Society and is being administered by the Macfarlane Trust. It is understood that the trustees are unable to divide the money equally amongst those 1200 haemophiliacs who are HIV-positive. It is also now known that at least 80 HIV-positive haemophiliacs have taken out writs against health authorities or drug companies.

The dilemmas created by the appearance of the AIDS virus are great, and the effect on those affected and those at risk are similar regardless of the source of their infection. The purpose of this chapter, however, has been to show that there are particular social and ethical issues which are peculiar to the situation of those with haemophilia who are HIV-positive or who have already developed AIDS. These issues deserve wider discussion.

Notes

This chapter is based on research carried out at the Haemophilia Reference Centre, Glasgow Royal Infirmary, and in the Department of Psychology, University of Stirling, and was supported by a grant from the Scottish Home and Health Department.

1.   I. Markova, C. D. Forbes and M. Inwood, 'The consumer's view of genetic counselling of haemophilia', *American Journal of Medicine and Genetics*, 17, (1984) pp. 741–52.
2.   D. Agle, H. Gluck and G. S. Pierce, 'The risk of AIDS: psychologic impact on haemophiliac population', *General Hospital Psychology*. vol. 9 (1987) pp. 11–17.
3.   R. Madhok, D. Campbell, A. Gracie *et al.*, 'Changes in Factor concentrate use subsequent to the publicity of AIDS in haemophiliacs', *Proceedings of the IInd International conference on AIDS*, Paris, 1986, p. 173.
4.   I. Markova, R. Lockyer and C. D. Forbes, 'Haemophilia: A survey of social issues', *Health Bulletin*, vol. 135 no. 4 (1977) pp. 177–82.
5.   P. A. Wilkie, 'Life Assurance, HIV seropositivity and Haemophilia', *Scottish Medical Journal*, 32 (1987) pp. 119–21.
6.   N. Wexler, 'Genetic Russian Roulette. The experience of being at risk for Huntington's Chorea', in S. Kessler (ed.), *Genetic counselling: Psychological dimensions* (New York: Academic Press, 1979) pp. 199–220.
7.   P. A. Wilkie, 'Psychological and ethical implications of HIV screening', in R. Madhok, C. D. Forbes and B. L. Evatt (eds) *Blood products and AIDS* (London: Chapman and Hall, 1987) pp. 201–16.

4 HIV and Pregnancy
Carole Ulanowsky and Brenda Almond

Recently in a hospital in an English provincial town where drugs, HIV infection and prostitution are problems associated with a distant world of fast city life, a young woman was encountering special difficulties with her first pregnancy. Clearly there were problems, but no diagnosis which seemed at all plausible had been offered. Only as she went into labour did a young woman physician make *her* first diagnosis of AIDS.

For the young mother, this was a totally unforeseen disaster – once the diagnosis was made, she was able to identify the source of the infection as a brief sexual encounter in the past, preceding the committed relationship in which she had embarked on pregnancy and childbirth. But at this stage, it was too late for the tragedy to be anything other than a double one, for the child was indeed born with HIV infection.

* * *

At the beginning of pregnancy, normal medical care includes the taking of a sample of blood and testing for a variety of conditions which it might be important for someone embarking on pregnancy, or for the physician caring for that person, to know about. These tests include checking for syphilis, rubella, hepatitis, jaundice and other possibilities; but few pregnant women are aware of the list of diseases which are being ruled out at this stage. There is no need for them to be, since for the vast majority the tests are negative. In addition, most of these conditions can be treated effectively, nor is stigma attached to positive findings in most of these cases. HIV infection, however, is seen as a special case, posing a special need for informed consent. At the same time, the notion of informed consent is being given a specially strong interpretation, in

41

which extensive counselling is regarded as a necessary condition if consent is to be considered truly 'informed'.

The burden of this counselling is likely, however, to be less medical than social and economic. Medically, HIV infection is a condition which cannot be cured, although there is evidence that some approaches to the problem may help maintain health longer. Beyond all doubt, the social and financial implications of a positive diagnosis are serious and important. Health and life insurance, mortgages and house purchase may all be affected. There may be problems for some types of employment and there are clearly likely to be difficulties on the personal level where the question of what to tell sexual partners or close relatives must loom large. A special practical fear on the part of a pregnant woman may be the loss of a sexual partner who is providing home and support for her. These are far from negligible considerations, and it is understandable, therefore, that some people might prefer to avoid knowledge of seropositivity.

Nevertheless the case that will be advanced here is that there are good reasons for HIV status to be established early in pregnancy; also that women who might become pregnant have stronger reasons than others to be sure that they are not seropositive. Our argument is not that testing should be forced on women who genuinely do not want it, but that it is useful and should be recommended to them – indeed, more strongly, that it should be regarded as routine except where special objections are expressed.

We would suggest, however, that consent should not be given a stronger interpretation than it is in the case of other tests made in the course of pregnancy. Nor should any counselling given be biased against consent. Our case is argued from several points of view: most importantly from that of the woman herself; but secondly, from the point of view of those involved in perinatal and maternity care; and thirdly, from a community perspective.

Because the problem of AIDS in the United States and in Western Europe has been particularly associated both in the public mind and in medical reality with certain defined groups: gay and bisexual males, intravenous (IV) drug users and haemophiliacs, it would be easy to underestimate the problem of young women contemplating or embarked on pregnancy.

But in New York the extent of HIV infection in the age-group most likely to be in this position is indicated by the fact that AIDS is already the leading cause of death for women aged between 20 and 29, and it is expected to become the leading cause of death for all women of child-bearing age in that city by 1990. In the United Kingdom there was a 26 per cent rise in the discovery of new HIV infection in pregnant women in 1987.[1]

Once the current and potential scale of the problem is appreciated, it becomes clear that this is not only a problem for a few individuals. Nevertheless, in considering the wider aspects, it is important to remember that the problem does come back in the end to individuals. This suggests that the issue should be looked at from three interlocking perspectives. First is the personal perspective: the considerations and concerns of a woman considering or in the early stages of pregnancy. Knowledge of seropositivity is emotionally traumatising for anyone in any situation, but for a woman the early stages of pregnancy are particularly precarious emotionally. Since counselling may well be involved, this is itself an issue for consideration: what advice should others give to a woman in this position? Does she need to know her HIV status? On what grounds should this information be sought or not sought? And, as far as others are concerned, on what grounds should it either not be established or, if available, be withheld?

Second is the perspective of the carer. Here a major consideration is the need for safety in perinatal situations. Obstetricians, gynaecologists and midwives have a duty to guard against the spread of infection from mother to baby and also from patient to patient. They also have a legitimate concern in relation to the risks they themselves run in perinatal care – risks which greatly exceed those of most other areas of medicine, since childbirth is a situation in which open wounds are the norm and in which practices such as the sampling of cord blood and the draining of mucus present special hazards. Is knowledge of the HIV status of their patients essential for their own security, and how will this knowledge, or the lack of it, affect practice in the maternity unit?

Third are the wider community aspects. It would be a narrow ethical perspective that confined attention to the individual patient, for, particularly in the case of a pregnant woman, two other individuals are likely to be directly involved:

one of these is, of course, the child she is carrying. The other is the father of the child. His position raises special considerations which will be discussed later. But apart from this immediate small circle, a new issue emerges here. For it has been argued that the public interest requires sound epidemiological data on the extent and spread of the disease, and that pregnant women provide the best possible source of this information. This is because they are healthy, sexually active and provide a more representative sample of the general population than do other groups who have been used for this purpose. In the case of this argument, the issue shifts from the interest of the woman to the interest of the community, so that the issue becomes: should pregnant women be treated as means to other people's ends?

In considering the set of problems that cluster round the issue of HIV and pregnancy, it would be easier to take this last issue first, for the questions involved are very different from those involved in the more directly personal areas.

MONITORING HIV INFECTION BY ANTENATAL SCREENING

It is important to distinguish between, on the one hand, the collection of epidemiological information that reveals facts relevant to named individuals and, on the other hand, anonymised testing, in which blood is not tested until all marks of identification other than place, age and patient category have been removed. In the latter case, it is difficult to see what valid objection can be raised to the practice.

One objection that is raised, however, by, amongst others, Dutch feminists, British midwives and the United Kingdom-based National Childbirth Trust is that the mere use of women for purposes not directly aimed at their personal good is offensive in itself. As a spokeswoman for the Royal College of Midwives put it 'Mothers should not be used in this way. There is no current justifiable reason to use them as a surveillance group. They attend antenatal clinics for specific reasons to do with the well-being of them and their babies'. She went on to say: 'Healthy mothers in this situation can hardly be called volunteers; but more as hostages to the need for new initiative to combat AIDS.'[2] But this emotive language can scarcely be justified in the case of genuinely anonymised testing. As the British Medical Association (BMA) Foundation for AIDS has recently argued to the contrary: the fact that no individual can be identified means that there cannot be any adverse consequences for the people from whom serum – already taken for other purposes – is exposed to this one extra test. For this reason, they suggest, specific consent is not required.[3]

In fact not all countries do take an antagonistic line, and this is why figures *are* available – from the United States, from some African countries, from Sweden and other European countries. These make it clear that the numbers of those affected are significant, at a level of significance which is recognised to justify screening in the case of other illnesses.

As far as the moral argument about the use of women for ends that are not their own is concerned, the fact is that this argument overlooks the way in which the interest of women bearing children is more closely and deeply connected with the community interest than is the case with any other sector of the community. To have a child is to commit oneself to society's future. Many women, seeing the issue as one of tackling a threat to that future, will be more than willing to make a contribution to the knowledge needed to maximise control of AIDS. So, while an explicit refusal should of course be respected, explicit consent should not be regarded as a moral requirement where anonymised testing is at issue.

THE PERSONAL DILEMMA

But the larger question remains: is ignorance the best policy for the individual? It must be accepted that many people – homosexuals, for example, or heterosexuals whose sexual life-style is varied and active – do not want to know if they are seropositive, since they are aware that even if they are, and nothing can be done about this medically, they may have a reasonable hope of some years of healthy and satisfying life, which could be blighted by knowledge of seropositivity.

But this argument, which raises many questions when it is advanced in connection with testing proposals for these groups, is particularly inadequate when applied to the case of women who are pregnant or contemplating pregnancy, for a number of reasons unique to this situation. To begin with, pregnancy and childbirth could well be precipitating factors as far as the development of AIDS is concerned.[4] Secondly, if AIDS is already present these factors may operate to accelerate illness.[5] And, most important of all, it may lead to the birth of a child with a poor medical prognosis, for there is a very considerable risk of children born to mothers who are HIV-positive being themselves HIV-positive and the progress of AIDS in children is faster than in the case of adults. Moreover, neonatal morbidity and mortality associated with perinatal HIV is high.[6]

For all these reasons, it is not true in the case of pregnancy, or of deciding whether or not to become pregnant, that knowledge can make no medical difference. In the United Kingdom, the fact of seropositivity is considered sufficient medically to provide a therapeutic reason for abortion,[7] and it may certainly deter many women from becoming pregnant if they have not already done so.

This is not, however, to pre-empt the decision about whether or not to proceed with pregnancy, for this must be the woman's alone. The question is rather whether such a decision is best made in ignorance. On the other side of the balance are more encouraging recent studies that suggest that a woman who is HIV-positive but otherwise healthy may give birth to a healthy baby and remain in good health herself. Earlier studies have tended, for a variety of reasons, to involve women whose overall health at the beginning of pregnancy was not good.[8] So some women will be prepared to accept the odds. For in this case, if a woman does not have any children already, the decision not to proceed is, in the present state of affairs as regards AIDS, a decision to remain childless. Knowing that her own prognosis is bad, or even anticipating a short life expectancy, may provide a very strong reason for a woman to seek fulfilment in motherhood.

One special case may be mentioned here: that of the seronegative partner of a man who is seropositive, possibly a haemophiliac who has contracted AIDS through contaminated blood products. In this case, a woman may have to consider incurring the risk of becoming HIV-positive herself in order to become pregnant; but she may judge this risk to be worthwhile in order to preserve something substantial from a relationship of love cut short by illness.

To make a decision of this nature, however, an individual needs to know not only the general position, but also her own HIV status. If the personal arguments for knowledge are valid, then it would clearly also be wrong for a counsellor to recommend that the choice be made in ignorance of the HIV status of those involved. It is noticeable, however, that counselling produces very different results in different contexts. In Sweden, for example, where great openness in sexual matters prevails, more than 99 per cent of pregnant women accept testing which is routinely offered them, while in the United Kingdom the figures are dramatically lower. Indeed in one study in a London clinic only nine out of an estimated 1500 women deemed of 'high risk' agreed to be tested.[9] This suggests a strong bias on the part of counsellors in the latter case, which is particularly significant in view of the Royal College of Midwives' demand for greatly increased expenditure on extended and in-depth counselling.[10]

Before leaving the matter of the situation as it appears from the individual woman's perspective, two other special points deserve attention. First, if the case for testing at the beginning of pregnancy is accepted, there is a need for speed in diagnosis, to allow a maximum of time for the difficult decision about possible termination. It is a disadvantage that HIV may take some time to detect by normal antibodies tests, a second test after a period of three months being recommended to confirm an initial negative finding, while antigen tests, which produce an immediate result, are not readily available. But this is not a good reason for abandoning any attempt to test at all, since this is a problem only for the small minority of cases where the infection has been newly contracted.

Secondly, it may be argued that tests in these circumstances may be more visible and less confidential than tests taken by individuals in circumstances of less pressure. The reason for a termination of pregnancy may emerge, bringing in its train all the consequences of publicity mentioned earlier. But this is not a necessary outcome, and the possibility is in any case not sufficient to outweigh the importance for the woman herself of what is at stake in this situation.

THE ISSUES FOR CARERS

These two last considerations point beyond the predicament of the pregnant woman and towards the surrounding circumstances – the social context within which decisions must be made. Most directly concerned are those with care responsibilities for pregnant women: physicians, midwives, nurses, counsellors. There are good reasons for beginning with their concern for safety since, as it turns out, this has considerable consequences for patients with HIV infection, for those deemed to be at risk of it, and for patients not thought to be at risk.

This may seem at first sight a surprising claim. But HIV/AIDS is already having a significant effect on antenatal, obstetric and paediatric care. At the antenatal stage, invasive investigative techniques which can give information about the foetus during the early weeks, detecting, for example, such conditions as Down's Syndrome, are in the case of women who are HIV-positive or considered to be 'at risk' likely to be avoided for fear of mixing maternal/foetal blood and secretions.[11]

Some clinicians, too, recommend Caesarian sections for such women in order to avoid possible transmission of the virus to the baby during normal vaginal labour, pending definitive results of investigations into the relative risks of modes of transmission from mother to baby.[12] However transmission may take place during pregnancy, *in utero*, through the placenta, or during the birth process itself. In the present state of knowledge, then, there is room for doubt as to whether Caesarian operations *do* reduce the risk of transmission of the virus.

The threat of HIV infection means, too, that a baby is likely to be delivered by a team wearing full protective clothing: cap, eye protection, mask, boots or overshoes, since 'body fluids may be shed unexpectedly and explosively.'[13] These precautions are recommended following labour and during the early post-partum period. Babies are to be handled with surgical gloves. These are recommended when touching the cord or doing heel-pricks, but also when changing diapers or dealing with vomit. Disposable paper tape-measures are proposed for measuring the infant's length and head circumference, and the use of speedy and efficient mouth-operated suction of mucus is not recommended.[14]

Because staff must see that other mothers and babies are protected, the Royal College of Obstetricians and Gynaecologists (RCOG)'s guidelines advise that women who are known to be HIV-positive or who are considered to be 'high risk' should be looked after apart from other mothers and babies during labour, delivery and immediately following the birth, and that they should not be allowed to handle other women's babies.

Care of the newborn also involves quite extreme precautionary measures. Investigative techniques to detect abnormal responses during labour – techniques which are highly specific and accurate – are likely to be abandoned in favour of less efficient but safer procedures in terms of avoiding transmission of the virus. Breast-feeding by HIV mothers is also discouraged, in view of the evidence of virus transmission by this means.[15]

In the United States some of these measures are recommended as universal practice, independently of the HIV risk, as a precaution against all blood-borne infections. In the United Kingdom, however, the natural childbirth movement has long campaigned for less technological management of birth and its aftermath, and would see unmediated human touch as important for both mother and baby. It may be, however, that informality of approach and setting must now be abandoned in general in maternity care, although in the United Kingdom it seems that the RCOG remains ambivalent on this issue, seeing stringent precautions as necessary in the case of women seen as 'high risk' for HIV, and unnecessary in other cases.

However the question of 'high risk' women and how they are to be identified is extremely controversial. Guide-lines vary with different bodies, but include: IV drug users and their sexual partners; partners of known HIV-positive men, such as some haemophiliacs; the partners of male bisexuals; prostitutes; women from African countries other than those bordering on the Mediterranean; women who have had sexual relations with men from these places, or whose sexual partners have had.[16] In Sweden the geographical regions are widened to include the United States, and recipients of blood transfusions since 1979 are also included.[17] A mere summary of these guide-lines is sufficient to show both that many apparently 'at risk' women will be wrongly presumed to be so, and also that many genuinely 'at risk' will fail to be identified by merely questioning.[18]

Compared with actually testing for evidence of HIV infection, it is clear that the 'risk' concept, when used so as to significantly affect a woman's perinatal care and that of her child, is a dubious and unreliable tool. In the case of genuine infection the precautions may unfortunately be necessary. Whether they are or not is a medical judgement on which we do not embark. But in the face of a mere possibility they are undoubtedly distasteful and extreme. Uncertainty about HIV status creates a situation of anomaly and paradox for patients and staff alike. Meanwhile contradictory messages are sent out: for example, it is recommended that a woman who needs resuscitation should be dealt with by staff who are wearing the correct clothing, proceeding 'according to the current recommended practice and standards', but 'it must be emphasised that maternal resuscitation should not be delayed whilst awaiting the appropriate equipment'.[19] If these measures are essential, then the tension can only be resolved by treating all untested women as infected or, as the term 'universal precautions' suggests, treating all women as potentially infectious.

Thus conclusion to be drawn from these complex safety considerations points in the same direction as the considerations to be taken into account by the patient herself: accurate knowledge of HIV status is important in the perinatal situation. But what of the broader position?

THE WIDER CONTEXT

A number of official statements about carers' responsibilities have defined these in terms which seem to limit them to the patient directly before them.[20] But, as the discussion so far has made clear, a woman on the threshold of pregnancy and child-birth is not an isolate or a unit. Intimately connected with her are child and, in most cases, husband or sexual partner. The narrower perspective has in fact never obtained in the case of maternity care, where mother and baby are regarded as a joint responsibility of the medical team.

As far as the well-being of the child is concerned, society in general has always declared its interest by, for example, making it a legal requirement on a pregnant woman to seek medical care. Without entering into the debate about abortion, it should be stated that the authors of this article have no doubt that a woman who has good reason not to proceed with a pregnancy should not be forced by others to do so. However they also believe that neither she nor her medical attendants can reach a rationally-based decision on this in relation to the HIV issue in ignorance of the facts in a particular situation.

To be taken into account here if the woman is in fact HIV-positive are not only the medical risks, but also the question of who is to care for the child if either or both parents are unlikely to survive its infancy.[21] It is important that medical advisers, counsellors or carers should not attempt to pre-empt the patient's right to consider these aspects, although paternalist attitudes in medicine, particularly in the area of gynaecology and obstetrics, are not uncommon. A British gynaecologist, for example, writes: 'What should *we* do about mothers-to-be with positive tests?' (our italics), going on to argue: 'There is at present no effective treatment to offer pregnant women with HIV infection'.[22] But it will be clear from the preceding section that there *is* much to be done medically with pregnancies taken to term, even apart from the important issue of termination.

And what, finally, of the sexual partner of the woman? He may or may not be the source of her infection and may or may not be HIV-positive. If he is not the source of her infection and is HIV-negative, then he is clearly at risk, and the question of disclosure to him is more sharply at issue than it is in the more general cases that have been discussed elsewhere by writers concerned with the issue of medical confidentiality.[23] This is because the pregnancy is in itself evidence of an active sexual relationship without protection, and would also be seen by most couples as a time to continue sexual relations without protection.

Clearly in such a case a woman must be urged to tell her sexual partner, and many women will, in any case, set their partners' health above their own more narrowly defined interest. (As far as physicians themselves are concerned, the situation could be regarded as one in which a breach of confidentiality would be justified where a woman was unwilling to take any kind of action herself, though not as one in which a new principle of a duty to inform had taken over from the usual need to preserve confidentiality.)

Such widening implications may lead to a reconsideration of the position so far argued for: that knowledge of HIV status should be sought where pregnancy is involved. So it is worth pointing out that, on the wider issue of testing for HIV infection, two main arguments are usually employed against it: (i) that in the absence of treatment or cure little can be done medically about the condition, and (ii) that the same advice must be given to people testing either positive or negative: that only 'safe sex' should be practised. But in the special case of pregnancy or a desire to become pregnant neither of these possible reasons for remaining in ignorance applies. There are crucial medical implications and, at least in order to become pregnant, barrier protection cannot be used.

So women contemplating pregnancy are in a particular 'need to know' situation and indeed, once this is more widely perceived by women themselves, it is possible that women will fill a vital role in the war against AIDS by bringing this disease out into the open, where it will be treated as a disease like any other, and not as a social embarrassment or stigmatising condition.

If this does not happen, the wider picture is bleaker still, as evidence from other parts of the world suggests. We may expect a dramatic impact on health and social services with huge economic costs and in the end, since this is a disease which attacks human beings in their reproductive function, an impact on birth patterns and a threat to population replacement. In the Third World these consequences, already visible, are beginning to be seen as posing a threat to economic and political stability.

In view of this, what is the way forward? Ultimately, of course, the prevention of perinatal transmission depends on protecting women of child-bearing age from HIV infection. In the absence of medical means of doing this, it is important that those with responsibility for health and sex education should move this issue to the front of education about HIV and AIDS.

(Currently such programmes in the United Kingdom, for example, give scant attention to the problem, and programmes of education for maternity do not mention AIDS.) So it is important for girls to understand the importance of knowing, before becoming pregnant, that they are not HIV-positive. It is important for them to understand, too, that if they are pregnant there are good reasons for them to establish their HIV status at the earliest possible stage.

As far as counselling and medical practice are concerned, those working in these fields should recognise the importance of testing for HIV infection as another routine procedure, except in those cases where a patient specifically objects.

This is not to set the community or the public interest above that of the individual woman. Far from it. For the worst thing that could happen to any young woman embarking on child-bearing is to reach the later stages of pregnancy and childbirth and *then* find out what she would so much have preferred to know earlier: that what would have been a single tragedy has been converted through ignorance into a double one.

Notes

1. John Osborne, 'Mothers and Babies', in Vicky Cosstick (ed.) *AIDS: Meeting the Community Challenge*, (Slough: St Paul's Publications, 1987) p. 33. A press report states that the percentage of HIV-positive women in the United Kingdom who have acquired the virus solely through sexual contact has risen from 11 per cent in 1985 to approximately 40 per cent in 1988 (*Guardian*, 14 Dec. 1988). The report adds that the typical profile of a woman diagnosed as HIV-positive in the United Kingdom is that she is white, in her twenties, working, and in a steady relationship.
2. General Secretary Ruth Ashton quoted in press release of Royal College of Midwives, London, 25 May 1988.
3. British Medical Association (BMA), 'BMA urges anonymous HIV testing', *Guardian*, 27 August 1988.
4. This is because pregnancy may alter cell-mediated immunity. See Howard Minkoff, 'Acquired Immunodeficiency Virus', *Journal of Nurse Midwifery* 31, 4 (July/August 1986) p. 191. However, in the case of asymptomatic women, recent studies would indicate a more

optimistic outcome: Dr Martha Rogers, Chief, Pediatric and Family Studies AIDS Program, CDC (private correspondence).

5. The position in relation to this claim is described in Catherine S. Peckham, Y. D. Sentura and A. E. Ades 'Obstetric and Perinatal Consequences of Human ImmunodeficiencyVirus (HIV) Infection: a review', *British Journal of Obstetrics and Gynaecology*, 94 (May 1987) p. 403.

6. Babies and young children infected with the virus *in utero* or during the process of labour progress to AIDS more rapidly than children who contract the virus at a later stage, for example through contaminated blood or blood products. See The National Swedish Board of Health and Welfare, 'HIV and AIDS in Care' (1988) p. 11. A transmission rate of around 30 per cent is indicated from clinical studies in several European countries currently collated by The Institute of Child Health, London. However, if the babies are tested at birth then the figure will appear to be much higher, since many will carry maternal antibodies well into the first year of life: Dr Jacqueline Mok, Edinburgh City Hospital, private communication.

7. BMA, 3rd BMA Statement on AIDS (1987)

8. G. B. Scott *et al.*, 'Mothers of infants with the Acquired Immuno-deficiency Syndrome. Evidence for both symptomatic and asymptomatic carriers', *Journal of the American Medical Association* 253, (1985), pp. 363–6 cited by C. S. Peckham *et al.* op. cit.

9. Ministry of Health and Social Affairs (Stockholm, 1988) p. 36. On the British example, see R. B. Heath *et al.*, 'Anonymous testing of women attending antenatal clinics for evidence of infection with HIV',*Lancet*, 8599 (June 1988) p. 1394. In the United States, testing in a Brooklyn Health Centre was offered to all pregnant women (that is, not simply those from high-risk groups) and was accepted by 40 per cent. See H. L. Minkoff, S. Holman, E. Bella, I. Delke, A. Fishbone and S. Landesman 'Routinely Offered Prenatal HIV Testing', *New England Journal of Medicine*, 319, no. 15 (October 1988).

10. See note 2 above.

11. Amniocentesis and Chorionic Villi sampling are two such tests. See advice given in The Royal College of Obstetricians and Gynaecologists' Report on Problems associated with AIDS in relation to Obstetrics and Gynaecology' 1988) p. 6, note 5.

12. See R. Chiodo, E. Ricchi, P. Costigliola, L. Michelacci, L. Bovicelli and P. Dallacosa, 'Vertical Transmission of HTLV III', *Lancet* 1, 739 (March 1986) p. 337.

13. RCOG 'Report on Problems associated with AIDS in relation to Obstetrics and Gynaecology', Appendix III.

14. Ibid.

15. Department of Health and Social Security, United Kingdom, 'HIV Infection, Breastfeeding and Human Milk Banking. Guide-lines for Doctors, Midwives, Chief Nursing Officers' (April 1988).

16. See Sheldon Landesman *et al.*, 'Serosurvey of Human Immuno-deficiency Virus Infection in Parturients', *Journal of the American Medical Association*, 19 (1988) p. 2703.

17. National Swedish Board of Health and Welfare, 'HIV and AIDS in Care' (1988) p. 19.
18. Sheldon Landsman *et al.*, 'Serosurvey of Human Immunodeficiency Virus Infection in Parturients', 2702. Authors report a study in an inner-city hospital in New York in which self-reporting and interviews failed to identify 42 per cent of HIV-positive women. Without the follow-up testing fo all individuals in this sample, five out of 12 women who were in fact HIV-positive would have gone undetected. This constitutes a sero-prevalence rate of 1.1 per cent in a group of women with 'no indentifiable risk factors'.
19. RCOG, 'Report on problems associated with AIDS in relation to Obstetrics and Gynaecology', p. 8.
20. For example, the Royal College of Nursing, London, is of the opinion that anonymous screening is an invasion of the integrity and privacy of the human being: testing, even if anonymised, should only be done with consent and with full counselling support. See letter to Chief Nursing Officer, Department of Health and Social Security, 'Response of RCN to DHSS Consultative document on anonymous screening' (August 1988).
21. Janine Railton, 'Women with Aids', in Vicky Cosstick (ed.), *AIDS: Meeting the Community Challenge*, p. 54.
22. John Osborne, 'Mothers and Babies', in Vicky Cosstick (ed.), *AIDS: Meeting the Community Challenge*, p. 33.
23. See, for example, Grant Gillett, Chapter 5. Also, Raanan Gillon, 'AIDS and Medical confidentiality', *British Medical Journal*, 294 (June 1987).

5 AIDS and Confidentiality: the Doctor's Dilemma

Grant Gillett

I

Does a doctor confronted by a patient with AIDS have a duty to maintain absolute confidentiality or could that doctor be considered to have some overriding duty to the sexual contacts of the AIDS sufferer? AIDS is a viral disease transmitted for the most part by sexual contact. It is fatal in the short or long term (that is, nine months to six years) in those infected people who go on to develop the full-blown form of the disease.

Let us say that a 39-year-old man goes to his family doctor with a dry persistent cough which has lasted three or four weeks and a 10-day history of night sweats. He admits that he is bisexually active. He is tested and found to have antibodies to HIV virus (indicating that he is infected with the virus that causes AIDS). In the setting of this clinical picture he must be considered to have the disease. He is told of his condition and also, in the course of a prolonged interview, of the risk to his wife and of the distinct possibility of his children aged one and three years being left without parents should she contract the disease. He refuses to allow her to be told of his condition. The doctor finally accedes to his demand for absolute confidentiality. After one or two initial illnesses which are successfully combatted he dies some 18 months later. Over the last few weeks of his life he relents on his former demands and allows his wife to be informed of his problem. She is tested and, though asymptomatic, is found to be antibody positive. A year later she goes to the doctor with fever, dry cough and loss of appetite. Distraught on behalf of her children, she bitterly accuses the doctor of having failed her and them by allowing

56

her husband to infect her when steps could have been taken to diminish the risk had she only known the truth.

In this case there is a powerful inclination to say that the wife is justified in her grievance. It seems just plain wrong for her doctor to sit back and allow her to fall victim to a fatal disease because of the wish of her husband. Against this intuition we can mobilise two powerful arguments, one deontological and the other utilitarian (of a rule- or restricted utilitarian type).[1]

(a) On a deontological view the practice of medicine will be guided by certain inviolate or absolute rules (not to harm, not to neglect the welfare of one's patients and so on). Among these will be respect for confidentiality. Faced with this inviolable principle the deontologically inclined physician will not disclose what he has been told in confidence – he will regard the tacit agreement not to disclose his patient's affairs to others as tantamount to a substantive promise which he cannot break. Against this, in the present case, we might urge his *prima facie* duty not to neglect the welfare of his other patient, the young man's wife. His inaction has contributed to her death. In response to this he could both defend the absolute duty to respect confidentiality in general and urge some version of the doctrine of double effect,[2] claiming that his clear duty was to honour his implicit vow of confidentiality but had the unfortunate effect, which he had foreseen as possible but not intended, that it caused the death of his other patient. One is inclined to offer an intuitive response, such as 'No moral duty is so binding that you can hazard another person's life in this manner.' It is a notorious feature of deontological systems that they involve conflicts of duties for which there exists no principled method of resolution.

(b) A rule-utilitarian doctor can mount a more convincing case. He can observe that confidentiality is a corner-stone of a successful AIDS practice. Lack of confidentiality can cause the irrational victimisation of sufferers by a poorly educated public who are prone to witch-hunts of all kinds. The detection and treatment of AIDS, and the consequent protection of that large group of people who have contacts with the patients being treated depends on the patients who seek medical advice believing that medical confidentiality is inviolate. If confidentiality were seen as a relative duty only, suspended or breached at the discretion of the doctor, then far fewer cases would present for detection and crucial guidance about diminishing risks of spread would not be obtained. This would lead to more people suffering and dying. It may be hard on a few, unfortunate enough to be involved with people like the recalcitrant young husband, but the general welfare can only be served by a compassionate but resolute refusal to abandon sound principles in the face of such cases. Many find this a convincing argument, but I will argue that it is superficial in the understanding of moral issues that it espouses.

II

Imagine, in order to soften the way for a rather less neatly argued position, a doctor confronted by a young man who has a scratched face and blood on his shirt and who wants to be checked for VD. In the course of the doctor's taking his history it emerges that he has forcibly raped two women and is worried that the second was a prostitute. He says to the doctor, 'Of course, I am telling you this in confidence, doc, because I know that you won't rat on me.' Producing a knife, he then says, 'See, this is the blade that I get them going with.' Rather troubled, the doctor takes samples and tells the young man that there is no evidence of VD. He tries to talk his patient into giving himself up for some kind of psychiatric treatment but the young man is adamant. It becomes clear that he has certain delusional and persecutional ideas. Two days later the doctor reads that his patient has been arrested because after leaving the surgery he raped and savagely mutilated a young women who, as a result, required emergency surgery for multiple wounds and remains in a critical condition.

Here we might well feel that any principle which dictates that it is the moral duty of the doctor to keep silent is wrong – but as yet no principles conflicting with or supplementing those above have been introduced. A possible loophole is introduced by the rapist's sadomasochism and probable psychosis but we need to spell out why this is relevant. In such a case we suspend our normal moral obligations to respect the avowed interests of the patient and claim that he is incompetent to make a responsible and informed assessment of his own interests and so we assume the right to make certain decisions on his behalf. In this case it would probably mean arranging for him to be given psychiatric help and for society to be protected from him in the meantime. Notice that he may have demonstrated a 'lucid' and 'intelligent' grasp of his predicament, *vis-à-vis* his own wish to avoid detection, but we discern that his instrumental rationality is deployed in service of a deep or moral insanity. His lack of awareness of the enormity of what he is doing to others counts as a sufficient basis to diagnose madness even in the face of astute inferential thought. He is insane because a normal person would never begin from the moral position he occupies and so his rights, including that to medical confidentiality, are suspended. He has moved outside the community of trust, mutual concern and non-malificence in which moral considerations for the preference of others have their proper place. It is not that one 'contracts in' to such a community,[3] nor that one in any sense volunteers,[4] but rather one is a *de facto* member of it by virtue of possessing those human sensitivities and vulnerabilities which give moral predicates their meaning and importance.[5] Such weight as one claims for one's own personal privileges and moral principles – such as the demand for confidentiality – is derived from a 'form of life' where the interpersonal transactions which define trust, respect, harm and so on, are in play (it is important that no particular ideological overlay has been grafted onto these). Of the insane rapist we can say that he has excluded himself from that moral community by the very fact of his violation of certain of its most basic tenets and assumptions. He has no right to demand a full place in that structure where morally significant human exchanges are operative because his behaviour and attitudes do not fit the place to which he pretends. We are, of course, not released from a *prima facie* duty to try and help him in his odious predicament but we cannot be expected to accord him the full privileges of a member of the moral community as he persists, for whatever reason, in callously turning his back on the constraints normally operative there (albeit, perhaps, without reflective malevolence in its more usual forms). So, in this case, confidentiality can be suspended for legitimate moral reasons. The mad rapist has moved beyond the pale in terms of normal moral interactions and though we may have a duty to try and restore him to full participation within that order we are also entitled to protect ourselves in the interim at the expense of those considerations that would apply to a normal person. Notice again that the boundaries of our attitudes are not arbitrary or merely conventional but involve our most basic human feelings and reactions to one another.[6]

III

We can now move from a case where insanity weights the decision in a certain direction to a case where the issues are more purely moral. Imagine that a 45-year-old man goes to see his family doctor and is also worried about a sexually transmitted disease. On being questioned he admits, in confidence, not only to intercourse with a series of prostitutes but also to forced sexual intercourse with his daughter. He is confident that she will not tell anyone what is happening because she is too ashamed and scared. After counselling he gives no sign of a wish to change his ways but rather continues to justify himself because of his wife's behaviour. The doctor later hears from the school psychological service that the daughter is showing some potentially serious emotional problems.

   Here, it seems to me, we have few compunctions about setting in motion that machinery to deal with child abuse, even though the sole source of our information is what was said, in medical confidence, by the father. The justification we might give for the doctor's actions is illuminating. We are concerned for the actual harm being done to the child, both physical and psychological, and we overturn the father's injunction to confidence in order to prevent further harm being done. In so doing we class the situation as one in which a *prima facie* moral claim can be suspended because of the actions and attitudes involved. I believe that we do so because we implicitly realise that here also the agent has acted in such a way as to put himself beyond the full play of moral consideration and to justify our witholding certain of his moral 'dues'. Confidentiality functions to allow the patient to be honest with the doctor and to put trust in him. Trust is (at least in part) a two-way thing and can only exist between morally sensitive human beings (this, of course, blurs a vast range of distinctions between degrees of sensitivity). A basic element of such moral attitudes is the responsiveness of the agents concerned to the moral features of human interactions. The legitimate expectation that a doctor be trustworthy and faithful to his patient's wishes regardless of the behaviour of that patient is undermined when the patient abuses the relationship so formed in ways which show a lack of these basic human reactions because it is just these reactions which ground the importance of confidentiality in general. Therefore, if the father in this example refuses to accept the enormity of what he is doing to his daughter, he thereby casts doubt upon his standing as a moral agent. Stated baldly, that sounds like an open warrant for moralistic medical paternalism, but I do not think it need be. In asking that his affairs be concealed from others, a person is demanding *either* the right to preserve himself from the harms that might befall him if the facts about his life were generally known, *or* that his sensitivity as an individual be respected and protected. On either count it is inconsistent for him to claim some moral justification for that demand when it is made solely with the aim of allowing him to inflict comparable disregard or harm upon another. By his implicit intention to use a position, which only remains tenable with the collusion of the doctor, callously to harm another individual, the father undermines the moral force of his own appeal. His case is only worsened by the fact that from any moral perspective he would be considered to have a special and protective obligation towards his own offspring.

IV

Implicit within what I have said is a reappraisal of the nature of medical confidentiality. I have argued that it is not to be treated as an absolute duty but is rather to rank among other *prima facie* duties and responsibilities of the doctor–patient relationship. Just as the performance of a life-saving procedure can be vetoed by the patient's choice to forgo treatment, even though it is a doctor's duty to strive for his patient's life, so each of these duties can be negated by certain considerations. One generally attempts to prevent a fatal illness overtaking a patient but in the case of a deformed neonate or an elderly and demented patient often the attempt is not made. In the case of confidentiality, I have claimed that we recognise the right of a patient to preserve his own personal life as inviolate. We accept that patients can and should share with a doctor details which it would not be right to disclose to other people But we must also recognise that implicit within this recognition is the assumption that the patient is one of us, morally speaking. Our attitude to him and his rights assumes that he is one of or a participant in a community of beings who matter (or are morally interacting individuals like himself to whom the same considerations apply). We could offer a superficial and rather gross systematisation of this assumption in the universalis-ability test.[7] The patient in the last two cases applies a standard to his own human concerns which he is not prepared to extend to others involved with him in relevant situations. We must therefore regard his moral demands as spurious; we are not at liberty to harm him but we are bound to see that his cynical abuse of the moral code within which he lives does not harm others. At this point it might be objected that we are on a 'slippery slope'. Will any moral transgression suffice to undermine the moral privileges of the patient? I do not think that this extreme conclusion can be supported from what I have said. Williams, remarking on the tendency to slide down 'slippery slopes'. observes, 'that requires that there should be some motive to move from one step to the next' and 'Possible cases are not enough, and the situation must have some other feature which means that those cases have to be confronted.'[8] Here we are not in such a position. Doctors in general have a strong tendency to protect their patients and keep their confidences. They require strong moral pressures to con-template doing otherwise. All I have sought to do is to make explicit the moral justification upon which these exceptions can be seen to rest. I have not spelled out any formal decision-making procedure whereby the right answer will be yielded in each case. Indeed it is possible that, whereas grounds and reasons recommending a certain course of action are the lifeblood of moral philosophy, such clear-cut principles and derivations are a 'will o' the wisp'.

Now we can return to the AIDS patient. From what I have said it becomes clear that it is only the moral intransigent who forces us to breach confidentiality. In most cases it will be possible to guide the patient into telling those who need to know or allowing them to be told (and where it is possible to so guide him it will be mandatory to involve him in an informed way). In the face of an expressed disregard for the harm being caused to those others concerned, we will be morally correct in abandoning what would otherwise be a binding obligation. We should and do feel the need to preserve and protect the already affected life of the potential victim of his deception and in this feeling we exhibit a sensitivity to moral rectitude. Of course, it is only the active sexual partners of the patient who are at risk and thus it is only to them that we and the patient have a moral duty (in this respect talk of 'society at large' is just rhetoric). If it is the case that sexual activity, as Nagel claims, involves a mutual openness in those who have intercourse,[9] one could plausibly argue that the cynical moral and interpersonal attitudes here evinced undermined the patient's sexual rights (assuming that people have such). The sexual activity of this individual is aberrant or perverted in the important respect that it involves a harmful duplicity towards or deception of his sexual partner. Whereas people may have a right to sexual fulfilment in general, they can hardly be said to have a right to perverted sexual fulfilment; but both Nagel's contentions and this talk of rights are contentious and it is outside my present brief to discuss them.

The doctor's obligation to inform, in the face of an enjoinder to keep his confidence, can, even if I am right, be seen to be restricted to those in actual danger and would in no wise extend to employers, friends or non-sexually interacting relatives of the patient or any other person with an even more peripheral interest. His duty extends only so far as to avert the actual harm that he can reasonably expect to arise from his keeping confidence.

Given the intransigent case, one further desideratum presents itself. I believe that doctors should be open with their patients and that therefore the doctor is bound to share his moral dilemma with the patient and inform him of his intention to breach confidentiality. I think he can legitimately claim a pre-emptive duty to prevent harm befalling his patients and should do so in the case of the abuse of others which the patient intends. It may be the case, with the insane rapist for instance, that the doctor will need to deceive in order to carry out his prevailing duty but this will hardly ever be so, and should, I believe, be regarded as unacceptable in general.

One thorny problem remains – the possible deleterious effect on the detection and treatment of AIDS if confidentiality is seen as only a relative principle in medical practice. Clearly, if the attitude were ever to take root that the medical profession could not be trusted to 'keep their mouths shut', then the feared effect would occur. I believe that where agencies and informal groups were told of the *only* grounds on which confidentiality would be breached and the *only* people who would be informed then this effect would not occur.

It seems to me that the remarkable intensification of one's sensitivity to personal and ethical values that is produced by contact with life-threatening or 'abyss' situations means that the cynical abuse of confidentiality by the patient which I have sought to address is likely to be both rare and transient. The greatest resource available to any of us in 'the valley of the shadow' is the closeness of those who will walk alongside us, and for many that will be a close spiritual and sexual partner. Confidentiality within the mutuality of that relationship rather than interpersonal dishonesty would thus seem to be vital to the welfare not only of the co-respondent but also of the patient himself as he struggles to cope with the disease that has him in its grip. To foster that welfare seems to me to be as close as a doctor can ever come to an absolute duty.

V POSTCRIPT: EPIDEMIOLOGICAL TESTING FOR HIV

The preceding discussion has been concerned with individual cases, but AIDS also raises an acute problem for epidemiology. The ethical requirement for consent to HIV testing and the hesitancy of many of those at risk about knowing whether or not they are affected together make a mockery of any epidemiological work on HIV infection and AIDS. To do good epidemiology in this area requires, of course, that one obtain blood samples from people not known or suspected to have HIV infection or AIDS and that depends on obtaining consent to a blood test which could potentially reveal one's HIV status. Thus we need to be clear about the ethical constraints on HIV testing and the nature and justification of requirements for consent and confidentiality.

The patient who is at risk from AIDS rightly feels that he has little to gain and much to lose if he is tested and found to be HIV-positive. We have, as I have noted, no effective therapy, so that he loses his normal expectation of longevity, and he is faced with an unenviable choice in his relations with others between candour with the risk of ostracisation and deceit with its strain and discomfort.

Testing for HIV does not necessarily involve a distinct procedure apart from taking blood for other purposes and therefore there is no requirement based on the physical act of testing that would normally be thought to require specific consent. Thus the sole reason for consent is the consequences of the knowledge that the particular individual concerned is HIV-positive and the ethical requirement that we make significant information about a person available to him. The worry is not completely avoided by not telling the patient because even the knowledge that there is a card which could enter play at any point and that carries such dire consequences for oneself is a significant thing for any person to have to live with.

Some would argue that true knowledge can never count as a harm but I think there is reason to doubt this with respect to the present issue. Thus it appears that we cannot avoid infringing ethical principles if we screen people for HIV antibodies without their consent but that we cannot get good epidemiological data if we insist on consent.

However there is a flaw in the argument. The harm for patient A arises from the fact that he has a positive HIV test. But what the researcher wants is a measure of how many unidentified and unnamed human beings are HIV-positive. Thus there is no conflict. Any sample she obtains from A need not be identifiable as being from A to serve her purposes. The ethical problems can therefore be 'finessed'. There is no invasion of A's privacy nor is there a potential harm to A, because nothing is known which can be traced to A. In this way the scientifically useful knowledge that x per cent of patients in the community are HIV-positive could be gained without infringing patients' rights or extracting ethically problematic knowledge about any given individual. The knowledge about A which we found reason to surround with norms of consent and confidentiality would not exist to be notified to or withheld from anybody including A himself.

If this recommendation were put into practice it would be true that blood from patients would have been used for research, but the lack of special ethical problems with that research would imply that a very general and non-informative form of consent could be gained, to the effect that the patient did not mind some of his blood being used anonymously for research. The lack of any material concern to the patient in the situation makes even this seem a little unnecessary. Thus I do not think that any ethical problem stands in the way of epidemiological research into HIV and AIDS, provided that the knowledge gained cannot conceivably be traced to any patient involved.

This conclusion has, however, prompted objections from doctors who have asked what they ought to do if they found, say, that one of a thousand patients tested was HIV-positive. Could such a doctor, in all conscience, let this individual go undetected and endanger other potential patients within the community? Must we not, therefore, be able to trace the sample and through it the affected individual? The arguments already advanced resolve this issue.

First, we have not sought permission to gain ethically problematic knowledge about a given patient. Second, we must seek that permission where we want to discover the HIV status of an individual. Third, the population is not really at risk and therefore does not need protecting. Fourth, we have served a research interest which has given us knowledge that we did not have that may ultimately benefit the whole community. If, as a result of such an exercise, we feel that a group ought to be tested to see which *individuals* are HIV-positive then we must ask each individual we propose to test as to whether he or she will agree. Some may well say 'no' and we will, perhaps, fail to find the affected individual but then we are no worse off than we would have been anyway and as researchers and scientists we (and therefore the members of our community) are much better off. Also we have avoided contravening the requirements of ethical medicine. However we may have to live with the fact that among a thousand people we have tested one, we know not who, is HIV-positive.

In any event the issue of confidentiality and the need for consent for HIV testing do not undermine epidemiological work provided certain ethical safeguards are met. We cannot, however, extend from anonymous testing to unconsented testing of patients as individuals or to the use of such individual information without attention to the very strict conditions under which, alone, confidentiality should be breached. The only basis for such a breach is and must remain, the risk of harm to another combined with a betrayal of those values which underpin our respect for confidentiality.

Notes

1. J. Rawls (1955) 'Two concepts of rules', *Philosophical Review*, 64, pp. 3–32.
2. J. Glover (1977) *Causing Death and Saving Lives* (London: Penguin).
3. As is suggested by Rawls (1971) in *A Theory of Justice* (Cambridge, Mass: Harvard University Press).
4. P. Foot (1978) 'Morality as a system of hypothetical imperatives', in *Virtues and Vices* (Oxford: Blackwell).
5. J. McDowell suggests that one imbibes the capacities for such judgements as part of the rule-following by which one acquires language, in 'Virtue and reason', *Monist*, 62(3), pp. 331–50.
6. I stress this point in order to distance the considerations that are guiding our judgement in this case from those situations in which an ideological framework has been used to override these very natural human reactions and provide a 'justification' for an inhuman moral code.
7. R. M. Hare (1965) *Freedom and Reason* (New York: OUP).
8. B. Williams (1986) 'Which slopes are slippery?' in M. Lockwood (ed.), *Moral Dilemmas in Modern Medicine* (Oxford: OUP).
9. T. Nagel (1979) 'Sexual perversion' in *Mortal Questions* (London: Cambridge University Press).

6 Autonomy, Welfare and the Treatment of AIDS
Roger Crisp

TWO PRINCIPLES

In most parts of the world, the vast majority of doctors have yet to treat large numbers of patients suffering from AIDS. Unfortunately this situation is unlikely to continue. Many people are already infected with the HIV virus, and it is spreading at an alarming rate.[1] It will be of small consolation to these doctors that AIDS does not raise any fundamentally novel ethical issues. For the old dilemmas will seem quite as intractable in their new context. Indeed some of the characteristics of AIDS – its prognosis and transmission, for example – seem to emphasise the starkness of the moral options open to those called upon to treat its sufferers.

In this chapter, I shall examine six important areas in which HIV and AIDS infection raise problems for the individual doctor. There are, of course, others. And AIDS gives rise also to questions in the spheres of law and social morality.[2] I hope that what I say may be relevant to these other issues, but it is not my intention to address them directly.

Ethical views are usually expressed from some perspective, be it Christian, Marxist, feminist or whatever. Two perspectives which dominate much ethical thought at present are those of liberalism and utilitarianism. These perspectives themselves rest on particular principles, liberalism on what I shall call the Autonomy Principle, and utilitarianism on the Welfare Principle. The principles may be stated loosely as follows:

The Autonomy Principle: one ought to respect the rights of autonomy and liberty.

The Welfare Principle: one ought to maximise welfare.

I shall call a person who advocates the former principle a liberal, and the latter a utilitarian. One of the striking things doctors, feel attracted by both. We want, on the one hand, to respect the rights of individuals to determine their own lives and, on the other, to fulfil our duties of benevolence towards either the individual involved, or other individuals.[3] Often it is this that gives rise to moral dilemmas in particular cases. For the two principles appear on occasion to counsel inconsistent courses of action.

In the cases I am about to discuss, I shall illustrate the position on each of a liberal and a utilitarian, as I have described them.[4] What is remarkable is that their practical conclusions are quite opposite in every case. I shall deal with each area in the form of a case-study. This is not only for the sake of clarity, but for a further reason which I shall later make clear. The cases, and indeed the positions taken on them, are over-simplified – and to that extent artificial – in order to emphasise their salient features.

SOME PROBLEMS

Paternalism

Alan is told by his doctor that the results of the tests he consented to have been returned, and that he is not, as far as she knows, HIV-positive.[5] Alan is known by the doctor to be at risk. He is an intravenous drug-user and engages in a great deal of casual gay sex. The doctor informs him of the dangers and how to avoid them, but Alan refuses to change his life style. He tells the doctor that he intends to continue both to practise unsafe sex and to share needles.

The liberal position. Alan has a right to determine how his own life should go. Once he has been informed, he should not be prevented in any way from continuing as before.

The utilitarian position. The doctor is required, in Alan's own interests, to try to prevent him from engaging in these life-threatening activities. She could, for example, approach those close to Alan and ask them to dissuade Alan from continuing.

The right to ignorance

Betty has been ill, and asks her doctor to carry out some blood-tests to ascertain the nature of her illness. She expressly requests that, should the tests show that she has AIDS, the doctor not tell her. The tests indicate that she has AIDS.

The liberal position. Betty has a right not to be informed of things which she does not wish to know. The doctor should not violate this right.

The utilitarian position. Betty cannot be cured of the disease, but there is treatment available which can alleviate its symptoms. For her to receive that treatment, it is necessary that she be told. If she is not treated, her own welfare and that of her friends and relations will be damaged for no good reason. There is also the possibility of risk to third parties.

Confidentiality

Colin, a bisexual married man, is advised by his doctor that he is HIV-positive. The doctor asks him whether he intends to inform his wife, or to practise only safe sex with her. Colin tells the doctor that he intends to do neither, and that he will continue to engage in unprotected sex with his wife.

The liberal position. Doctors must not breach their professional obligations of confidentiality. The doctor may attempt to persuade Colin to change his mind, but on no account must he inform the wife.

The utilitarian position. If Colin refuses to yield to persuasion, his wife should be informed by the doctor as soon as possible.

The rights of practitioners

Doreen, an intravenous drug-user, was warned by her doctor not to share needles. She ignored this advice, and is now HIV-positive. The doctor feels that Doreen brought the disease upon herself, and also that he is not called upon to risk his own life for his patients. Therefore he wishes to reject Doreen as a patient.

The liberal position. Other things being equal, the doctor has a right to decide whom he shall treat, just as a publican has a right as to whom he shall serve. The doctor may therefore refrain from treating Doreen, even if we think this callous.

The utilitarian position. What people deserve is irrelevant here. The doctor must act in the interersts of his patient, unless the risk is very great. It is not great. Therefore Doreen should be treated by the doctor.

Consent

Eric's doctor suspects that Eric may have anaemia, and Eric therefore agrees to a blood-sample being taken. After Eric has left the surgery, the local health authority contacts the doctor to ask whether it may use the blood-samples taken at the surgery that day in random and anonymous blood-testing for HIV. The tests are aimed solely at obtaining statistics concerning the spread of the virus in the area.

The liberal position. Eric has a right over his body and its parts. If the doctor believes that the blood should be released to the authority for testing, Eric must be informed and his consent obtained.

The utilitarian position. Eric will not know that his blood has been tested, and because the tests are randomised and anonymous, no harm can come to him even if he is HIV-positive. Therefore the doctor can agree immediately to the health authority's request.

The rights of patients

Fiona is a General Practitioner, who has become HIV-positive through sexual contact with a bisexual man. Although she is aware that many of her patients would prefer to register with another doctor than be treated by her, she intends to continue to practise without informing her patients of her condition.

The liberal position. Patients have a right to be informed of any condition of their doctors which may threaten their lives. Fiona should either cease to practise, or advise her patients so that they can make an informed choice.

The utilitarian position. The patients are very unlikely to be harmed if treated by Fiona. She will certainly suffer greatly should she have to cease practising, or see the number of her patients fall drastically. Therefore she should continue to practise, and keep her condition hidden for as long as possible.

These, then, are the areas on which I want to focus. Clearly some moral issues arise in more than one area. Consent, for example, is relevant not only in the case of Eric, but also in every other case apart from that of Doreen. But in general the various problems in each area are sufficiently distinct to justify my differentiating them as I have.

POSSIBLE SOLUTIONS

The cases I have discussed will present themselves to most people as moral dilemmas. This is because, as was noted, most of us are neither pure liberals nor pure utilitarians. But this puts us in a quandary whenever the two principles – the Autonomy and Welfare Principles – conflict. Sometimes, of course, they will not. Often welfare can be maximised most efficiently by respecting a person's autonomy ('only *she* knows what she really wants'). But in the six cases above, there is a conflict. What is the concerned doctor to do in such cases?

One suggestion might be that she reflect upon which principle she wishes to hold onto, and which to reject. She must decide whether, in fact, she is a liberal or a utilitarian, just as a football supporter, who has cheered equally loudly for United and City throughout the season, must finally make up his mind at which end of the ground to stand in a local Derby.

This policy would have at least one desirable consequence. Moral decision making would be far less taxing. The doctor has only to work out what her chosen principle requires in each case, and carry it out, ignoring the opposing principle altogether. But it is clear also that this kind of decision making pays for its simplicity the price of insensitivity.

It often helps, when examining moral principles, to apply them to the situation of a single individual, at the prudential or *intra*personal level. It enables one to focus one's intuitions on the values underlying the principles, and to avoid complications arising from trade-offs or their prohibition in cases involving more than one person, at the *inter*personal level.

First, then, consider what it would be like for me to run my life according to the Autonomy Principle. Most of the time, all would go well. I would presumably use my autonomy to further my welfare (allowing the Welfare Principle lexical posteriority, that is, application once the Autonomy Principle has been respected) and a satisfactory level of welfare seems anyway to be a necessary condition of autonomy. But there are times when strict application of the Autonomy Principle is likely to make my life go worse. For example, in some areas of my life, I may wish to hand over control to other people, in order to avoid anxiety to myself. I may have atrocious taste in clothes, and ask someone else to choose what will suit me best. If I do not do this, I will spend much of the time when I am in public fretting over my appearance. Or I may wish to deepen a close personal relationship. This would require assuming certain obligations which would diminish my autonomy, even if only in a small degree. But my life would go better were I to deepen the relationship.

Now consider a life lived on the Welfare Principle. Again, of course, in most cases there would be no conflict with the directives of the Autonomy Principle. I am generally in the best position to decide what is best for myself, and handing over too much control to others can be dangerous. They may have in mind not benefiting me, but using me for their own ends. Again, however, in certain cases the Welfare Principle looks quite mistaken. Imagine that you are twenty-two years of age. You are approached by a committee of the elder members of your family. They tell you that they are willing to take over the running of your life. They will give you the right job, introduce you to the most interesting people, supply you with the best books to read, and so on. Looking back on your life so far, and all the wrong turns that you have made, you realise that the committee, the members of which you trust implicitly, are certain to run your life better than you can. Nevertheless you would be foolish to accept this proposal, even if the committee were to run your life more efficiently. For a person's life to be well worth living requires that to a substantial degree the life be led by that person and not by others. The Welfare Principle alone will not suffice in the prudential sphere.

This example can guide us towards a solution of the problems raised by the conflicts that arise between the recommendations of the two principles in particular cases. We should see autonomy as *itself part of welfare*. It is not just having a good job, fascinating friends and enjoyable hobbies that make my life worth living, but the very leading of that life itself. Both the liberal and the utilitarian, as I have characterised them, have an impoverished conception of welfare. This leads the liberal to exaggerate the value of autonomy, and the utilitarian to ignore it. But a richer conception of welfare, in which control over the central parts of one's life features as itself a substantive value, enables one to avoid the apparent conflict.

The liberal and the utilitarian may remain unconvinced by my argument for a richer conception of welfare. Adopting the lines taken by, on the one hand, classical utilitarians and, on the other, most modern utilitarians, they may claim that welfare is *either* a certain mental state, such as pleasure, or a number of mental states, such as pleasure and aesthetic contemplation; *or* the fulfilment of desires, actual or corrected in the light of rationality. For a conception of welfare to play any important part in moral thinking requires that values be commensurable, in order that trade-offs of one good for another can be made in particular cases. The objection to my claim is that I have set up autonomy as itself an intrinsic value, a thing good in itself, an end. And because I refuse to take a reductionist stance towards autonomy (explaining its value in terms of mental states and/or the fulfilment of desire) I am left with unacceptable incommensurabilities which will paralyse moral thinking.[6]

One rejoinder here might be to accept full incommensurability of values, but deny that this rules out moral thinking.[7] But this strikes me as an unhappy response. For if autonomy and, say, pleasure are incommensurable in the way that, for instance, the height and smell of a rose are incommensurable, it is indeed hard to see how we could engage in serious moral thinking. Moral thinking, including that of doctors, has to proceed on the assumption that there are certain answers to moral questions which are better than others, whereas, if the Autonomy and Welfare Principles never make any contact, we shall be left in the same quandary as that which the richer conception of welfare was to help us avoid.

A more promising reply would be to question the very assumption on which the objection rests. This is the view that, if one argues that there are several things which are valuable in themselves, comparisons are impossible. The nature of practical reasoning itself throws this view into doubt. Consider another prudential case. I have received my pay-cheque, and am deciding on what to spend it. My alternatives are a bathroom-heater or a series of Spanish evening classes. What happens when I am deciding? Surely not that I reduce the alternatives to some common substratum, such as pleasure or the fulfilment of my desires, and then balance them to find the more weighty? Rather, I adduce *considerations* in favour of each alternative: the bathroom was freezing last winter; I have a cold coming on; I profited greatly from learning Italian two years ago; I have nothing better to do on Wednesday nights; and so on. Then, in the light of these considerations, I *judge* the alternatives and come to a decision. If we agree that this analysis of practical reasoning is, for the most part, accurate, then the assumption on which the objection rests must be false. And if my prudential thinking is not paralysed by a pluralism of values, then I see no reason why my moral thinking should be.

MORAL DECISIONS

I have suggested, then, that with a richer conception of welfare, including autonomy as itself a substantive value, we may be able to move towards a resolution of certain moral dilemmas which are likely to face those involved in the treatment of HIV and AIDS. Let me now return briefly to the six areas of conflict I described, in order to see whether there is substance in the suggestion.

Paternalism: is the doctor to prevent Alan from risking his life?

Bearing in mind the committee example above, it may seem obvious that the liberal position on this issue is correct. But this would be too swift. In that case, you were asked to surrender control of your life for all time. If we take a more global view of autonomy, seeing it as a value in a temporally extended fashion, we can see that it can sometimes be restricted for the sake of autonomy itself. I may restrain you temporarily from committing suicide, and later you may thank me for doing so. For you have a life you would not otherwise have had, over which you have control. It may be that the doctor *should* interfere, at least temporarily. The decision must depend on the further facts of the case, which the doctor must do her best to ascertain. Is Alan angry at the virus, and thus not thinking straight at the moment? Or is his decision a reasoned one – his identity is so bound up with the way he lives that he feels that to change his life would be to change his identity? If the latter is the case, then I believe that Alan's autonomy should be respected. Even in the former case, the doctor should take steps to interfere warily and only after much reflection.

The right to ignorance: should Betty be told that she is suffering from AIDS?

In certain cases of cancer, doctors argue that the patient should not be told of her illness on the ground that it lessens the chance of recovery. In the case of AIDS, however, there is no chance of recovery. But patients can be kept well to some degree in cases of both terminal cancer and AIDS. Effective treatment requires some understanding by the patient of the nature of the disease, in order that she may participate in active interventions. For example, treatment using the drug Zidovudine (AZT) would prolong Betty's life and improve its quality. Also relevant is that with appropriate support and counselling patients usually adapt well to their illness, even when they have previously taken a very negative attitude towards it. Given all this, and taking into account also the facts that Betty's accelerated deterioration is likely to cause great upset to her family and friends, that she may put others at risk, and that she will find out anyway that she has the disease, I am inclined to say that she should be informed, tactfully and gently, of the result of the tests.[8]

Confidentiality: should Colin's wife be informed?

When we contemplate the position of this couple in isolation from the rest of society, it is quite clear that the wife should be told. Colin's autonomy is important, but not to the extent that he should be enabled to put the life of another person at serious risk. But there is a further (utilitarian) argument in favour of confidentiality, based on a broader view of the case.[9] If it becomes known that doctors breach confidentiality, it is said, other people with AIDS will be more reluctant to come forward, and this will cause more harm overall. This argument rests, of course, on certain empirical assumptions. And these assumptions are almost certainly false. First, doctors will be called upon to breach their obligations only in a very few cases, where they have been unable to persuade the patient to do her duty. (Doctors are already permitted or required to do this in certain cases.) Second, there is still a strong self-interested reason to motivate people with AIDS to visit doctors, even if they are worried about breaches of confidentiality. Dying from AIDS is extremely unpleasant, and dying without professional medical care even more so. (Of course, this latter reason will not apply to those who are merely HIV-positive.)

The rights of practitioners: should the doctor treat Doreen?

It might be said that Doreen will suffer no harm by being transferred to another doctor, whereas, if the doctor is required to treat her, his autonomy will be violated. Both of these claims are incorrect. The role of doctors as pillars of the community should not be ignored. Doreen may well hold her doctor in high regard, as a respected and sympathetic figure. To be rejected by him when she is in dire need of comfort and support could be very damaging. But what of the doctor's autonomy? Medicine is a profession, and becoming a professional requires one to surrender one's moral autonomy in the sphere of the profession in order to place oneself under the special obligations of the profession. It is unlikely to be morally appropriate for a doctor to act in a way inconsistent with his professional duty. He exercised his autonomy in entering that profession, and it is partly doctors' readiness to abide by the requirements of their profession that makes them so valuable to the community. Now it may be said that even a doctor is not required to give up his life for his patients. There is much in this. But the doctor here is not being asked to give up his life. He is being asked to place his life at *some* risk. But his professional obligations of course require him to put his life at some risk. Here the risk of infection is so small, especially if the doctor takes precautions, that it is clear that he is obliged to treat Doreen.

Consent: can Eric's blood be tested?

Autonomy does involve certain rights of self-ownership. A doctor cannot remove important organs from Eric's body against his will in order to benefit a number of others. But do these rights extend to small amounts of blood which have anyway been transferred to others? I think not. If I find that my hairdresser has been sweeping up hair-clippings at the end of the day, washing them, and using them as stuffing for cushions for his dog, it would be absurd for me to insist that he seek my permission first. Whatever happens to the hair-clippings, my autonomy remains unviolated. The same applies with the blood-sample, as long as (a) the tests are randomised and anonymous (to protect Eric's rights to confidentiality and ignorance); and (b) Eric has not specifically requested that such tests not be carried out. It is worth pointing out that it is already common practice for blood to be tested in this way for various other infections. It might be argued that Eric's consent should anyway be sought.[10] But if his autonomy will not be violated by the tests, this will be merely a waste of time and resources which could be put to better use elsewhere. There are also the social benefits accruing from greater knowledge of the epidemiology of the disease to be considered.

The rights of patients: should Fiona tell her patients that she is HIV-positive?

It will help to clarify the issues in this case if we imagine another, similar in all relevant respects except that the patient is objecting to the doctor because she is black. We should not be any more inclined to sympathise with this patient's wish if she claims that black doctors are more likely than white doctors to have contracted a tropical disease, and thus to be putting her life at risk. The probabilities here are so small as to expose what is said as a patent rationalisation of prejudice. Given that there is sufficient public education about HIV and AIDS, those of Fiona's patients who deserted her would be acting out of prejudice. And to say that autonomy requires that one be able to harm another out of prejudice is mere cant. Fiona may continue her work without informing her patients. Her condition is not their business. If she were involved in invasive surgery, however, the case would be different. Here the perceived risk would be closer to the actual risk and, since the risks are at present difficult to assess, I am readier to say that Fiona should either refrain from carrying out such surgery or make clear her position to the patient.

Using the richer conception of welfare, then, I have been able to approach in a more balanced way the problems raised. I do not expect the reader to agree with the substance of all the proposed solutions above. What I am attempting primarily is to suggest a methodology which will not ignore the importance of either autonomy or welfare.

I want to conclude with a general point about our approach to practical moral questions. This point is especially relevant to those called upon to treat people with AIDS. For they will, as I have said, meet old problems in new guises. My aim in this paper has been the modest one of removing an obstacle to moral thinking. I do not expect that a doctor will be able to take the notion of welfare I have advanced and use it as just another tool of the trade, like a stethoscope. Moral decisions are of such complexity that they are not made, and cannot be made, solely on the basis of a number of explicit, statable principles. Doctors should well be able to appreciate this, for it seems that there is a strong analogy between their methods of diagnosis and moral decision making.[11] Doctors take the symptoms of the patient as considerations, and judge in the light of them. This capacity to judge in such spheres is found in what Aristotle calls *aisthesis* – 'perception' or 'sensitivity'.[12] Medical sensitivity comes with medical experience. We are likely to find less practised doctors consulting more experienced colleagues on unusual cases. Likewise, the capacity to make moral decisions is partly a matter of sensitivity to relevant considerations. And moral *aisthesis* also comes through experience.[13] This was my second reason for employing case studies above. By contemplating hypothetical cases, elaborating upon them, and discussing them with others, doctors will sharpen their sensitivity to the actual moral considerations in the dilemmas which are bound to occur in their everyday practice.[14] AIDS, being so new and so terrible, poses a great challenge not only to the medical but to the ethical capacities of doctors. Serious moral thinking about the disease can serve only to prepare them for the deluge of suffering they are about to face.

Notes

I owe many of the thoughts in this chapter to discussions with James Griffin. I am grateful for comments on earlier drafts to Brenda Almond, Anthony Crisp, Anthony Grayling, Gabriele Taylor and two anonymous referees for the *Journal of Medical Ethics*.

1.   Scientific advisers have told the British government to expect between 10 000 and 30 000 cases of AIDS by 1992. See S. Connor and S. Kingman, 'AIDS cases set to grow fifteenfold', *New Scientist*, no. 1641 1988, pp. 23–4.

2.   Some of the legal issues are discussed in M. Kirby, 'AIDS legislation – turning up the heat?', *Journal of Medical Ethics*, 1986, 12. Some social issues are covered in R. Mohr, 'AIDS, gays, and state coercion', *Bioethics*, 1987, 1.

3.   The most well-known exponent of the two principles contemporaneously is, of course, J. S. Mill, in his *On Liberty* and *Utilitarianism*. Many efforts have been made to find a consistent position in Mill. A good survey is M. Strasser, 'Mill and the utility of liberty', *Philosophical Quarterly*, 1984, 34. See especially J. Gray, *Mill On Liberty: A Defence* (London: Routledge & Kegan Paul, 1983).

4.   The names I have attached to each problem are not intended to favour either the liberal or the utilitarian perspective. They are merely those most commonly used to demarcate the sphere of discussion. Nor am I to be interpreted as claiming that any 'real' liberal or utilitarian must advocate the positions in the text. The positions as well as the cases are simplified to bring out the main point of my argument.

5.   One must be clear as to the distinction between HIV (the Human Immunodeficiency Virus) and full-blown AIDS (Acquired Immune

Deficiency Syndrome). The ethical implications of any particular case may well depend on this distinction.

6.   I argue the case for non-reductionism in 'Quality of life in health care', in G. Gillett (ed.), *Medicine and Moral Reasoning* (Oxford: Oxford University Press, 1989).

7.   See I. Berlin, 'Two concepts of liberty', *Four Concepts of Liberty* (Oxford: Oxford University Press, 1979); C. Taylor 'The diversity of goods', in A. Sen and B. Williams (eds), *Utilitarianism and Beyond* (Cambridge: Cambridge University Press, 1982).

8.   See M. Strasser, 'Mill and the right to remain uninformed', *Journal of Medicine and Philosophy*, 1986, 11.

9.   See also Chapter 5.

10. Gillon R. 'Testing for HIV without permission', *British Medical Journal*, 1987; 294, pp. 821ff.

11. The analogy is an ancient one. It is considered by Plato (see, for example, *Republic*, 331e1–334b6); and adopted by Aristotle (see, for example, *Nicomachean Ethics*, VI. 1, 1138b21–32).

12. *Nicomachean Ethics*, II. 9, 1109b21–3; VI. 8, 1142a23–30.

13. *Nicomachean Ethics*, II. 1, 1103a31–b2; VI. 8, 1142a11–20; VI. 11, 1143b6–14; X. 9, 1181a19–b12. See also J. McDowell, 'Are moral requirements hypothetical imperatives?', *Proceedings of the Aristotelian Society*, supplementary vol., 1978, 52; 'Virtue and reason', *The Monist*, 1979, 62; 'The role of *eudaimonia* in Aristotle's ethics', in A. Rorty (ed.), *Essays on Aristotle's Ethics* (Berkeley and Los Angeles: University of California Press, 1980); 'Aesthetic value, objectivity, and the fabric of the world', in E. Schaper (ed.), *Pleasure, Preference and Value* (Cambridge: Cambridge University Press, 1983).

14. I discuss the ethical training of those who treat the terminally ill in 'A good death: who best to bring it?', *Bioethics*, 1987, 1.

Part II

The Community Perspective

7 The Role of the Media and the Reporting of AIDS

Julian Meldrum

This chapter is based on a talk given in 1986, criticising the behaviour of sections of the British press. In this area, perhaps more than any other covered in this book, events have moved on and both medical perspectives and social concerns have shifted. I think this is interesting in itself, demonstrating some of the problems in tackling 'inaccurate' coverage, so in revising the talk for publication I have tried not to allow the benefit of hindsight to alter my original judgements.[1] I would like to add that I think it is far too easy to condemn people now for underestimating the seriousness of AIDS when it first appeared, and to talk and write as though the consensus (that a new virus, HIV, is the cause of AIDS) was instantly and painlessly reached. In fact, small but influential sections of the American gay community (and in particular the *New York Native* newspaper) have clung to any other theory on offer, rather than accept what appeared to me, as to most informed European, Canadian and Australian observers by 1983, to be the most likely explanation. This account also brings out forcefully the fact that my own activism grew from a perception that AIDS, although serious, was a potentially manageable problem in which community action could still make a real difference. Had I accepted some of the more dire assessments – that 'everyone must be infected by now' and so on – I would not have become involved in the way that I did.

The impact of media coverage of any subject depends on the interaction of several factors, including the previous knowledge of the readers or audience; the content of the message; the credibility or otherwise of the journalists; and the reactions of people with whom the reader or viewer goes on to discuss what they believe they have read, seen or heard. In my talk I began by giving the background to my own involvement with AIDS as a gay activist who helped to set up the first British voluntary AIDS organisation. I then went on to talk about the media and the tradition of treatment of homosexuals and perceptions of homosexuals against which AIDS emerged into the public mind, as a homosexually-associated condition. One of the key issues is that the mainstream media have an overwhelming perception of their public as being heterosexual. I did not think it enough to criticise 'bad' coverage, and so I put forward an interpretation of 'the public interest' in AIDS as one of the criteria for defining how best to go forward. Having set out such a standard, I went on to present a series of examples of media coverage and the problems they raised, ending with some comments on what is left unsaid in the media, and why it matters.

THE MAKING OF AN ACTIVIST

I first became involved in the community response to AIDS in May 1983, through a public meeting organised by what is now London Lesbian and Gay Switchboard, with money from the Greater London Council and the Health Education Council. For the previous couple of years, my main aim in life had been to establish the Hall-Carpenter Archives, a lesbian and gay charity which assembled one of the best British collections of recent press cuttings referring to homosexuality.[2]

For the Hall-Carpenter Archives, I cut out and photocopied in the summer of 1981 an article from *The Times* of London which reported that a 'rare cancer' had been identified among gay men in New York and California, and that a task force on Kaposi's Sarcoma and Opportunistic Infections was being set up by the Centers for Disease Control (CDC) in Atlanta, Georgia. Conditioned as I was to think of cancers as caused by chemical environmental agents, I thought the problem as remote as the numbers were small.

During 1982, when, according to Dr Jim Curran of CDC, most scientists in the field became convinced that AIDS (as it had been dubbed after angry and mostly gay protests against nicknames like 'gay compromise syndrome' and 'gay-related immune deficiency') had a transmissible basis and was following an epidemic pattern, there were articles in the medical journals and in the gay press but little else, certainly on this side of the Atlantic. (The first American network coverage took less than two minutes on NBC news on 16 June 1982, reporting that AIDS was probably a sexually transmitted disease, since a number of gay men with AIDS in California had named each other as sexual partners.)[3] The article which did most to bring AIDS into focus for me appeared in the Toronto monthly, *The Body Politic*, at the end of 1982. The authors demystified AIDS through a comparison with hepatitis B. They argued (mistakenly) that the epidemic was levelling off in the United States and that, while AIDS would be a serious problem, it was a limited one.

When I attended that public meeting in May 1983, the speakers included Mel Rosen, then Director of New York's Gay Men's Health Crisis, and Martyn Butler, the founder and promoter of the Terrence Higgins Trust. I was struck most forcefully by the evidence – put forward by Dr Ian Weller of the Middlesex Hospital – for a retroviral cause of AIDS with a carrier state, a long incubation period, a minority of those infected progressing to AIDS, poorly transmissible, and with no evidence that the incidence had reached its peak in the USA, although it would surely do so before many years were out. I did some crude calculations and concluded that by the time there were half a dozen cases of AIDS in Britain – as indeed there then were – there must be several hundred to a thousand people infected, and infectious, with the causal agent. If the American peak were at five to ten thousand cases a year, which then seemed quite possible, the British numbers would be just into four figures. Although I did not and do not believe that all gay men are doomed, and although it was clear that this problem was not confined to gay men, it was still only a matter of time before someone I knew died horribly, slowly, prematurely, from this disease. My first reaction was to cry. I had known several Americans as friends and sexual partners and, while I was very unlikely to die, I might be infected. They might be infected. There was no cause to panic, I insisted, but I did panic. I rushed around pestering all sorts of people, had a week of mostly sleepless nights, and ended up locked out of my own flat, having lost the keys on Friday. (Along the way I saw a video recording of the first credible TV documentary, a 'Horizon' programme made in mid-1982 and shown at the end of April 1983. Credible, that is, apart from some extrapolated exponential curves, setting a date when the entire population of the world would have AIDS!)

The next public meeting was a smaller affair, from which the present Terrence Higgins Trust evolved; a meeting held above the London Apprentice public house near Old Street. The three months which followed were hectic. I felt, I think we all felt, that everything should have been done the day before anyone suggested it. There were painful clashes of personality within the group, a voluntary organisation with no formal constitution, no funding, and with a sense of confronting a crisis. It was a very bruising set-up, and I am sure I inflicted as much pain as I received. After three months I lost my temper and left. However, by that time, other people had been brought in and it was set on the road towards a proper constitution, charitable status, and a clearly defined educational and social service role, as distinct from raising money for research, which had been Martyn Butler's first objective.

I then moved into journalism. My first major article on AIDS appeared in the January 1984 issue of *Gay Times*, and from July 1984 for two years I was a regular columnist for *Capital Gay*, writing almost every week on AIDS. I attended conferences on AIDS in the United States, in Amsterdam, London, Brighton and Newcastle. From the end of 1985, I again worked with the Terrence Higgins Trust (leaving to take up employment in 1986).

THE ROLE OF THE MEDIA

One definition of the role of the media is to entertain and to inform the public. The central problem with the mass media in relation to AIDS has been the definition of AIDS – by historical accident – as a peculiar property of gay men; and the exclusion of gay men from that public. The historical accident is that, although, worldwide, most transmission of HIV is and has probably always been heterosexual, the epidemic first came to medical notice when it affected gay men in the United States.

The exclusion of gay men from the 'public' is symbolised in Britain by the fact that the BBC has never yet broadcast a programme identifiably for lesbians and/or gay men. Even Channel Four, standard-bearer for 'minority interest programming' is only just getting round to the idea (for 1989). There are, admittedly, gay pages in the London events listings magazines, *City Limits* and *Time Out*, erratic sightings in the *Guardian*, and a bold but abortive attempt by the *New Statesman* to integrate lesbian and gay journalism into a left-wing political mainstream. Elsewhere, lesbians and gay men are defined as 'the other', and often as a threatening 'other', which cannot be trusted in times of crisis. As Antony Vass has shown, in his thought-provoking and interesting study, *AIDS: a Plague in Us*, there are double standards at work.

At the same time there appear to be few things more entertaining than grave misfortunes which occur to other people. The British popular press is especially fond of little stories that teach us that deviants come to a sticky end, especially those deviants who are suspected of enjoying themselves more than the average reader might, or of evading some of the burdens of responsibility – the crumbling house, the tiresome children, the financial worries, the loveless marriage, the dreary job – that so many endure as the social cost of living.

Stories about AIDS as a plague on gay men fit neatly into a long tradition in which the popular press is free to report on any criminal or spy who may be identified as homosexual, but colludes in a conspiracy of silence where sports players, trade union leaders, senior academics and doctors, 'mainstream' artists and actors, or esteemed Fleet Street journalists are concerned. Indeed the apparent exceptions prove only to confirm the rule. Rock Hudson became a gay man when he was seen as dying from AIDS. Ten years ago the editor of *Gay News* became a minor national figure when he was prosecuted for blasphemy. The politician Jeremy Thorpe became a byword for homosexuality when a former boy-friend denounced him in court. Billie-Jean King and Martina Navratilova became lesbians when the press tired of them. (This treatment of homosexuality is not an isolated problem. 'Black crime' – meaning street crimes by black people against whites – is a precise analogue of the more recent 'gay plague'.)

SETTING AN AGENDA

Although the media amplify and give expression to anti-homosexual and other kinds of prejudice, in doing so they reflect wider problems of power distribution in our soceity, problems for which they are not solely responsible. In criticising the media, we imply that there is scope for social change, and seek to use the media as an instrument to bring about such change. So, in addition to providing entertainment and information, the media can set the agenda for the development of public policy and influence the actions of those who do have power in our society. In approaching the role of the media in relation to AIDS we therefore need an idea of where the public interest lies, and of how public policy should evolve. Such an idea must clearly be founded on the best available medical knowledge. Unfortunately, while this knowledge accumulates over time, it does not always become clearer, and it inevitably reflects social values that may themselves be disputed.

I shall say little about the medical perspectives on AIDS, save that, for the foreseeable future, we are facing a condition that is not medically controllable either through vaccines or drugs, and although research on both fronts has to proceed urgently, the only things that can influence the course of the epidemic over the next few years are information on how the virus is transmitted – and how it is not – and education to convey that information to people at most risk either of infection or of passing the virus on.

I think that the aims of social policy should be to minimise transmission of the virus, through education, while preserving civil liberties and the integrity of society, with a minimal degree of stigmatisation of those affected by AIDS. As Sir Donald Acheson, Chief Medical Officer at the British Department of Health, said in 1986: 'Stigma, as we have seen in relation to epilepsy, TB and leprosy, is an enemy of public policy. It does nothing to help in dealing with real problems.'[4]

THE TROUBLE WITH THE NEWS

I shall now turn to some examples of actual coverage, and try to show how they conflict with those values and obstruct the kinds of social policy I would wish to see.

AIDS first became newsworthy, at least as far as the British newspapers were concerned, in relation to blood transfusion. The first front-page news reports were on Sunday, 1 May 1983, when the *Mail on Sunday* ran a banner headline, 'Hospitals using killer blood', referring to two people said to have contracted AIDS as a result of being treated for haemophilia with imported Factor VIII concentrate. The author asserted that there were 'safe supplies' of Factor VIII available for the asking from European suppliers. If this had been true – either that supplies were available, or that they were safe – then the paper might have been justified in printing the story that it did in the way that it did. As it happens, there were no such supplies available, at least not in the amounts that would be needed for the British market. (And, with hindsight, they might not have been so much safer than the American ones. Many Australians with haemophilia became infected with HIV in spite of a blood transfusion service that had been nationally self-sufficient for years, and entirely reliant on volunteer donors.)[5] The particular article was the subject of a Press Council complaint, brought by Dr Peter Jones for the Haemophilia Society, which was upheld, rightly I think, albeit a year after being brought. Another case which I think even more sharply showed the difference in values and the definition of AIDS as a problem only when it affects and is seen to affect heterosexuals, was an article in the *Daily Mail*, given the headline 'Second man dies of AIDS in Britain', which actually referred to the second death of a person with haemophilia.

While the newspaper reader is assumed never to engage in homosexual acts, anyone could have an accident and need a blood transfusion. Thus, despite the relative insignificance of blood transfusion as a mode of transmission of AIDS in the United States and other Western countries, it was the threat to public confidence in the blood transfusion service that riveted the attention of the media and has been the primary incentive to develop a governmental response. By November 1984, the

Department of Health became aware that HIV had been transmitted through blood transfusions from British donors. Fearing a public relations disaster, they moved to set up an 'Expert Advisory Group' on AIDS, in which the blood transfusion services were heavily represented, although in the developments that followed some corrective action was taken when it became clear that the major problems lay outside the blood transfusion service.

We have heard already of the dangers of 'casual transmission'. The media are obsessed by the phrase because, as with blood transfusion, it suggests that anybody can be at risk in a particularly dramatic way. I would like to draw attention to some of the ways that spurious 'casual transmission' stories can be generated, as most of the stories have been spurious. I am especially concerned that this can happen as a result of breaches of confidentiality and attempts to plaster over these breaches once they have come about. In fact, if we look at things in a wider perspective, even if there were half a dozen cases where it was unambiguously clear that casual transmission of HIV had occurred, this would not alter the fact that the very confinement of AIDS overall and for a long period in the United States demonstrates the pattern that Tony Pinching describes in Chapter 2. We knew that, even before the virus had been isolated; disproportionate attention even to real examples would be a public disservice as a distraction from the central realities of the problem. Casual transmission will not be a major means by which the virus is spread.

The association of transmission with taboo behaviours – sex and drug-taking – has, in itself, obvious potential to generate scares if confidentiality is not guaranteed to people identified as HIV-infected. In 1983, the first casual transmission scare occurred in the USA – an editorial in the *Journal of the American Medical Association* discussed the possibility of household transmission of the AIDS agent through intimate personal contact. America panicked. A dustman, a family man, working in an area of New York with many drug-users, came down with AIDS. The idea was put about that he had caught AIDS through needlestick injury. The refuse workers were on the point of striking. It was later reported that the man admitted, virtually on his deathbed, that he had been bisexual, and had had homosexual contacts, which seemed a more likely explanation.[6]

Several police officers have contracted AIDS in the United States (and at least one or two in Britain). In America, health insurance is often provided in occupational schemes. Disgracefully, some of these schemes have tried to avoid paying out for people with AIDS, arguing in the case of policemen, say, that, as their illness was contracted through immoral or unprofessional acts, they should not be covered. Part of the explanation for the pressure for 'spacesuits' for policemen has come from solidarity felt towards officers who have been threatened in this way. Other policemen would rather give the benefit of any conceivable doubt to their colleagues than face a day when an occupationally acquired infection is excluded from cover. A similar case and problem exists in relation to the armed forces, at least in the United States, where several servicemen who have developed AIDS were initially denied invalidity discharges and benefits, being threatened instead with dishonourable discharges, on account of having 'behaved dishonourably'. Although these cases have been fought, and won, in the courts, the armed forces still have not lost that mentality. In 1985, they began testing all recruits, refusing those who were positive, and compiled lists of names and addresses which were allegedly provided to public health officials.

While it is well known that homosexual relationships are often hidden, heterosexual relationships are sometimes denied as well. There is the potential for a whole genre of stories of AIDS being contracted from neighbours in the system whereby income support for unemployed women is cut substantially when they are 'cohabiting' with men, particularly when you consider that the drug-users who are among the people at highest risk are often impoverished, living on bad housing estates and playing cat-and-mouse games with the Department of Social Security.

Even laboratory workers would be better off if their HIV infections were, or were thought to be, occupationally acquired. The *Sun* actually published an editorial in 1985 calling for the suspension from work of a seropositive laboratory worker who handled blood samples at a provincial hospital; even the National Health Service has taken a long time to develop anything like a credible policy on the employment of antibody-positive workers; and HIV infection due to employers' negligence could net substantial compensation awards, even in British courts.

The case which really burst onto the public consciousness, in 1985, related to the death of a chaplain at Chelmsford prison. The publicity which arose from that incident did more than anything else to convince the mass of journalists outside Fleet Street that something needed to be done about professional ethics and the behaviour of some of their colleagues in reporting on AIDS. According to an article by Simon Heffer in *Medical News* (28 February 1985), national press stringers were hanging around Chelmsford for the week or two prior to the death, waiting for the chaplain to die in order to spring the story on the world. Keith Dovkants, whose report in the London *Evening Standard* on 31 January 1985 was the first to do this, is, significantly, a news reporter and not a medical reporter; most of the coverage was by news reporters. Health correspondents working on the same papers have told me of their disgust over what was done. The principal fault with that report and those that followed was that they implied either that the chaplain had sexual relationships with many or most of the young men in his charge, or that the virus was casually transmissible. They talked about contacts amongst former inmates being chased up by the Communicable Disease Surveillance Centre, which was utter nonsense. It is quite understandable in that context that the prison officers behaved as they did in blocking movement in and out of the jail, and of course that *was* newsworthy.

A further problem which has arisen recently in at least two cases is the false identification of individuals as 'AIDS victims'. One case of a man terminally ill at one of the major hospitals in London which treats people with AIDS became a front page story in the *Sun* about a well-known pop singer visiting the man. The story claimed firstly that the man had AIDS, secondly that in order to visit him the singer had to don weird protective clothing. According to the hospital, as reported in *Capital Gay* at the time, they would not barrier-nurse people with AIDS; secondly, the man in question had leukaemia and not AIDS; thirdly, the singer had not visited the hospital; and finally, the story appeared to have arisen out of the newspaper commissioning someone to pose as a health worker, wandering around a ward, asking people what their diagnosis might be and inferring that it was an AIDS ward she had stumbled into, putting two and two together and making up to a thousand pounds which I understand was then the going rate for 'before and after' pictures of people with AIDS paid by certain tabloids. (A Press Council ruling in 1987 accepted the pop singer's word that he had not visited, but otherwise declined to take the hospital's side against the newspaper and the agency that had sold the story to them.)[7]

The second case is perhaps a more serious one, showing that it is not only journalists who manufacture stories. A man was found dead near a railway line in South London and the evidence suggested he had been strangled. The local police knew through contact with the man and his flatmate that the flatmate may have been antibody-positive for HIV. They informed the workers at the mortuary where the body was taken, who – according to the police – refused to have anything to do with the body or to let anyone else touch it for two or three weeks. The police were unable to get a pathologist to do an autopsy. One of the minor ironies of this situation was that the man had been tested and found to be HIV antibody-negative. The police none the less insisted to the press three times that the dead man had AIDS. The stories that appeared in the local press highlighted a police theory that the man had been killed in revenge for having transmitted AIDS to a former sexual partner. (The man later convicted of the murder, who was reported as being antibody-positive, had killed before and made attempts on the lives of other gay men.) What can possibly be done about such behaviour by public officials?

Finally, I would like to raise the issue of what is left unsaid and why it matters. One thing is that, worldwide, HIV is predominantly a heterosexually transmitted infection and that it is being heterosexually transmitted, albeit on a relatively small scale, in this country. There is no reason to believe that in the long term it will be confined to the groups currently identified with it, either in this country or in any other country. One of the biggest problems of the obsession with particular modes of transmission (random transmission through blood transfusion and supposed 'casual transmission') is that it distracts the public from the massive evidence from the bulk of the cases. The limitation of news media as a mode of education and communication is very sharply exposed; what is new is news, but the background to it does not have anything like the same news value. The only solution is for responsible organisations to take it upon themselves to launch effective advertising campaigns, and I do not consider the first British Health Department newspaper campaign to fit into this category. I think that television with its far greater impact is infinitely more important and needs to be brought into play without further delay.

We need to move away from the division into 'us' and 'them'; we need among other things to encourage people to think how they themselves would behave if they were identified as carriers of a sexually transmitted, poorly transmissible but probably lifelong infection, and to try and promote a greater sense of community between those directly affected and those, which includes the rest of us, who are going to be indirectly affected by this disease over the years to come.

POSTSCRIPT: POSITIVE APPROACHES WIN OUT

At the time of the talk, in 1986, I had been involved in efforts to get the British National Union of Journalists to censure unprofessional behaviour by its members and to issue guide-lines (which they did). However I now believe this to have been of limited value, as the NUJ suffers from an extremely weak industrial position, especially in relation to Rupert Murdoch's News International Group, which incorporated the worst offenders against taste and journalistic ethics.[8] The Press Council, a self-regulatory newspaper industry body, has been equally useless. If some of my fears concerning British press coverage have not yet been realised, the reason is probably the effort put in by the BBC and ITV (the national television and radio networks), which ran an intensive week of public education broadcasts, documentaries, discussions and other items during March 1987, shortly after the distribution by the Department of Health to every household of an information leaflet, succeeding I believe in raising the level of background knowledge that could be assumed by journalists to the point where (a) most no longer felt it necessary to explain that AIDS was short for 'the gay plague' and (b) some of the sillier casual contagion stories were no longer credible or of interest to the readers. Whether this state of 'enlightenment' can be maintained, as the Health Education Authority (HEA) hopes, through low-key informative advertising in newspapers remains to be seen. What is, however, most encouraging is the positive role increasingly taken by people with AIDS themselves, supported by organisations such as Frontliners, in presenting their very individual experience to remind us of our common humanity.

Notes

1. Andrew Scott, 'AIDS and the experts', *New Scientist*, 5 March 1987, is an excellent review of some of the problems of assessing 'the truth' about a developing area of knowledge.
2. Lisa Power, 'Voices in my ear', in Bob Cant and Susan Hemmings (eds), *Radical Records: Thirty years of lesbian and gay history* (London: Routledge & Kegan Paul, 1988) especially p. 152. This refers to the first public meeting in the course of a discussion of London Lesbian and Gay Switchboard's response to AIDS and its influence as a model for the development of the Terrence Higgins Trust.
3. My source for this is a presentation by Robert Bazell, NBC science correspondent, at the conference 'AIDS: Impact on Public Policy' held at the New York Hilton, 28–30 May 1986, co-sponsored by New York State Department of Health and the Milbank Foundation.
4. Sir Donald Acheson made these remarks at the New York State Milbank Foundation conference mentioned above.
5. See, for example, an Australian Government news release dated 15 November 1985, issued in the name of the Federal Minister for Health, Dr Neal Blewett, headed 'AIDS Grant to Haemophilia Federation', which reported that 30 per cent of people with severe haemophilia tested in Sydney had at that time been found to be antibody-positive for HIV.
6. For a discussion of early American coverage, refer to Rodger Streitmatter in *The Quill*, May 1984, pp. 22–7, 'AIDS: It's just a matter of time' and, from a very different perspective, Dorothy Nelkin, 'AIDS in the Media', in *Science in the Streets: Report of the Twentieth Century Fund Task Force on the Communication of Scientific Risk*, 1984. Coverage in some other countries, and especially in Australia,

has been even more extraordinary, as discussed by Dennis Altman in *AIDS and the New Puritanism* (New York: Doubleday; London: Pluto Press, 1986); and as catalogued by Robert French in his bibliography, *Mossies could spread AIDS: Australian media references on AIDS, 1981–1985* (Sydney: Gay History Project, PO Box 9, Darlinghurst 2010, Australia, 1986).

7.   'Le Bon did not visit pop band manager in hospital', *UK Press Gazette*, 20 April 1987.

8.   Nicholas de Jongh, 'When the real disease is press distortion', *Guardian*, 14 April 1986. The editor of the *Sun* is quoted replying to a complaint by an NUJ officer about a report on AIDS: 'The NUJ's views on Aids in general are of no interest to the Sun and have no bearing on our decisions on what to publish.'

8 AIDS: Risks and Discrimination

Michael Smithurst

'There is a virus which is sexually transmitted and which is causing an estimated 500,000 deaths a year. Most of those infected by the virus, or family of related viruses, suffer no ill-effects, and these antibody-positive individuals show little or no sign that they have been infected; but in some cases there are other factors operating, the etiology is speculative and unclear, but factors such as a general poor condition of health, inadequate and improper diet, smoking, stress, can enter into the picture, and the virus, with these, forms a necessary link in a chain of cause and effect which makes an otherwise harmless lesion become a horrible cancer causing slow death in almost all who suffer it, unless their condition gets an early diagnosis. Happily or otherwise, this illness affects a despised group of people who are accorded less than equal rights as members of society. The viruses in question are types 16 and 18 of the papilloma virus. The mode of transmission is heterosexual genital intercourse, and the victims are called women.

The press has not labelled cervical cancer the straight plague, the gloomy plague, or whatever the appropriate antonym is. Barrier methods of contraception can obviate the evil almost entirely, but unaccountably, the government has not placed any minatory advertisements in national newspapers (though what designation the coiners of 'rectal intercourse' would have found for vaginal intercourse I will not venture to speculate), and, though the prepuce is criminally implicated in the transfer of the virus, I have not heard that any politician has recommended the rounding-up of millions of practising heterosexual males and the institution of a programme of compulsory circumcision.'[1]

With this bid for irony I began some remarks to the Social

99

Values Research Centre's conference on 'Ethical and Social Perspectives on AIDS' in June 1986. It got the laugh aimed at, but since I cannot make the points I want to and sustain the tone, I will not now let it stand unquoted in cold print. I was intending, of course, to undercut the recriminative implication of the supposed connection with male homosexuality that was then, and seems to me still, a main feature of the popular and media-based conception of AIDS. I could have as well made the point by saying that the majority of the world's cases of HIV infection have been contracted through heterosexual genital intercourse,[2] and that the 'Western' perception of the infection as a primarily homosexual-related phenomenon is a consequence of simplistic extrapolation from data recording the initial spread of a sexually transmitted disease in certain big city populations. It is as if an unwary viewer were to take the first ten results after close of polling as the pattern of the completed returns.

Cervical cancer is a sexually transmitted disease that presently kills and disables a larger number of people than does AIDS. Why then the different receptions accorded these diseases? There are some half-way rational grounds for making a distinction. Cervical cancer is more of a known quantity, prognoses are more certain, constructive courses of action are more definitely known, and half the human race, the male half, are at no risk from it. Is it the 'incurability' of AIDS that adversely structures the public perception? It cannot be that alone, for cancers and other diseases can often be seen to be fatal well before the death of the patient, and for parts of the world's population many illnesses are *de facto* incurable.

Should the difference be attributed to the widespread and false belief that HIV is highly infectious, and to the, misleading, representation of AIDS as a 'blood disease' and the consequent jittery perception of it as a 'contagion'? These implications are a staple of the press and broadcasting media accounts and no amount of authoritative denial seems able to modify them. It is not only the popular press (which unabashedly publishes known falsehood on the subject), but the ordinary daily reporting of 'quality' newspapers that feeds unjustified fear. Take this small item, randomly picked from the *Guardian*[3] at time of writing, and typical of hundreds of similar items in the British press. It is headlined 'Aids

Precaution', and says: 'Anglican churches will no longer pass the communion cup among worshippers as a precaution against Aids, Bishop Misaeri Karuma, of Namirembe, said yesterday. He said the decision had been taken by his diocesan council in view of the widespread concern about Aids in Uganda.' There is in fact no evidence that HIV can be transmitted by use of a drinking vessel. Such a thing is quite unknown and there are no good reasons to anticipate it happening. The *Guardian* does not tell its readers that the 'precaution' is no precaution at all, it just puts yet another *suggestio falsi* into circulation.

That misinformation engenders fear and that fear creates, or more likely, liberates, prejudice does not need arguing. Its victims are sometimes people with AIDS, but usually those who are HIV-positive or who are thought possibly to be so. Typical recent news items include the following: a woman sacked from her job because her husband is HIV-positive; another driven by the attacks of neighbours from her home because a three-year old daughter is antibody-positive; parents organising a boycott of a school because three haemophiliac brothers are pupils there, and so on. A recent radio programme on AIDS featured an interview with a health service worker, a married man with children, who had become antibody-positive. He had been open about the matter with acquaintances and with his employer. Attempts had been made to sack him, and then to force him into early retirement. He knew of moves to sack others, individuals who were falsely rumoured to be antibody-positive. His trade union was making no effort to fight his case. The interviewer asked, 'What advice would you give to others in the same situation?' and he replied, 'Say absolutely nothing. It will ruin your career, and your family life, and it will destroy your friendships.'

Does not everyone have a right of prudent self-protection? They do, but prudence is a rational notion, and what counts as rational here? We have become like the woman in the Thurber cartoon who, cringing in her armchair and looking upwards, is afraid that the electricity is leaking. One can attempt to correct misinformation, but what is to be done when the public refuses to learn? In a television symposium on AIDS a restaurant owner declared roundly that he would sack any waiter believed to be HIV-positive. Medical experts explained to him that the virus could not be transmitted in the preparation and serving of food, that there was no risk, that they themselves had eaten food prepared by people having the virus, and so on, but nothing could move him. His intransigence was supported by a journalist, George Gale, who said that, for his part, he would not eat in a restaurant of which he had heard that a member of the staff was HIV-positive, and put this robust question to his critics: 'Why should I take a risk, however small?' The question deserves an answer.

On the immediate point at issue (whether to dine in a restaurant . . .) the answer is simply that there is no risk, and the fears are *altogether* misplaced. But a more interesting issue lies here. What is one to say of the case where a very small risk of harm exists, and people justify discriminatory courses of action by appealing to the right of self-preservation? Now if one is talking about risks however small, then the circumstances of a life that seeks to guard against such risk would be preposterous. No one keeps a surgical mask permanently over his face, though doing so could on some occasion save someone from fatal infection. Bound by such precautions one becomes like the Jain monk, who, with veil across his mouth and a brush to sweep the insects from his path, seeks to do harm to no living creature. In a sense, Mr Gale's question is insincere. Everyone crosses a road, drives a car, takes aeroplane flights, and so on, and rarely perceives these activities under the tendentious heading of 'taking a risk'.

Suppose that someone, however unreasonably, determines to guard against very low risk in some specific connection. Is that an objective that can itself be pursued without risk? I think not. I do not know how to prove it, but I think one could propose a general principle to the effect that in circumstances of very low risk a sufficiently complex overview of the situation will always reveal factors indicating that one will encounter higher risk in other directions.

Let me explain this with an illustration. *Toxicara canis* has sometimes caused blindness or eye-damage in children and it can be transmitted through consumption of dog faeces. The danger of it is frequently cited as a justification for presently proliferating bye-laws restricting dog walking in parks and attempting to enforce the collection of faeces by dog owners. However, *toxicara canis* is rarely contracted, and even more rarely does it cause blindness (less than one case a year in the

United Kingdom). Proportionate to the population and the number of dogs, the risk is very small. Are we neverthless obliged, or at least entitled, to guard against it? It might seem so, until one remembers that there are other things to put into the utilitarian balance. For example, given the very low probabilities one is dealing with, may not a general practice of pooper-scooping with attendant accidents, be as much or more likely to lead here or there to the ingestion of some small amount of canine faeces? Further, will not quite a few people, especially town dwellers, the infirm and the elderly, be deterred from dog keeping by draconian legislation on where the mutt can deposit it?

Now several curious studies have established that pet owning is beneficial to mental and physical health. For instance, it has been found that people hospitalised with cardiac arrest are more likely to recover when they have a pet to return home to. Controls showed that wife, children, or other human companion awaiting, made no difference to recovery rates, but that a dog or budgerigar markedly increased the patient's survival chances. I cannot vouch for the research here but it has been publicised often enough. One cannot calculate whether the blights set on an individual's freedom to walk his dog generate a risk equal to that of *toxicara canis* or one somewhat larger. We are dealing with infinitesimal imponderables. My suspicion is that very small risk, and vigilance to guard against it, will always tend to land one in this sort of situation. The answer to 'Why should I take a risk however small?' is that seriously to decline to do so involves entering into a tissue of inconveniences and absurdities attached to an indeterminate number of other, mostly unforeseen, very small risks.

Let me now repeat that the *existing evidence* is that ordinary human intercourse, bar the sexual, is not a circumstance of very low risk of HIV infection, but one of no risk at all. Anxiety interjects the thought that the scientists may be wrong. Perhaps they may, but the possibility of their being wrong should not be equated with one's being at risk. If the thought is that evidence is not total and expertise is not immune from error, then anything can be hung on that speculation. Error can be in any direction. No evidence of risk means no known risk. Any speculative fear that anyone chooses to add is just free play of imagination.

The discriminations made against HIV-positive people are unjustified. If the hostility has no rational basis and nevertheless fiercely resists correction, what then fires it? I think that any glance over the British popular newspapers of recent years shows that the dread of AIDS is in large part a reflection of that culture's dread of homosexuality. The connection between AIDS and homosexuality (that is, the false connection made by ignoring international patterns of the spread of HIV and focusing on statistics of its initial spread in Europe and the United States) is a product of this fear and a God-given propaganda vehicle for those keen to foster it. Ignorance has given illiberal opinion a weapon that it uses constantly, and increasingly without fear of contradiction.

An example can be drawn from the political advertising in the British general election of 1987. For the United Kingdom, it represented a frightening degradation of public standards. A translation of some innocent and solemn Scandinavian booklet explaining homosexuality to schoolchildren was shown on Conservative party hoardings which asked 'Is this what you want for your children?' Other items of 'fag-baiting', with the standard references to AIDS, featured in the Conservative campaign. The Labour Party and the Liberal Party (both committed by decisions at their party conferences to legal equality for homosexuals and to anti-discrimination legislation) stayed quite silent. A government pamphlet published in early 1987 and called 'AIDS, Some Questions and Answers, Facts for Teachers, Lecturers and Youth Workers' says this: 'As it appears that homosexual intercourse [*sic*] has been of major significance in the transmission of HIV in this country, particular care needs to be taken in dealing with the subject of homosexuality especially in schools.' Some months after the publication of this document, the Minister of Education, Kenneth Baker, issued a directive that any schoolteacher reported as 'saying anything sympathetic about homosexuality' [*sic*] should have the report relayed to school governors, who will be 'obliged to consider the case'.[4]

Common misunderstanding or prejudice makes the connection between AIDS and homosexuality simply through a myopic look at the statistics. Mr Baker and his colleagues propound an argument. The premises are (1) that anal intercourse *qua* anal is particularly implicated in the spread of

AIDS, and (2) that, for the most part, anal intercourse is a homosexual act, and is the form typically taken by 'homosexual intercourse'. The implied conclusion is that homosexuality should be 'discouraged'. The first premiss is probably false, and the second almost certainly is. The first is *prima facie* incompatible with the African data on AIDS and the gender ratios of distribution. It has been suggested that people in the countries concerned are especially given to heterosexual anal intercourse. It is also said that they deny this, and treat the question with some amusement. Evidence is not extensive, but in one investigation 'the researchers concluded that frequency of intercourse with different partners was more important than type of intercourse'.[5] If frequency and variety of sexual contacts is sufficient explanation of the patterns of transmission found, it is superfluous to make the hypothesis of a particular homosexual susceptibility because of anal intercourse.[6]

As to the second premiss, the most extensive British investigation of male homosexual behaviour found that only 32 per cent of subjects regularly had anal intercourse, and noted that 'a large proportion of the sample do not like anal intercourse at all'[7] (General caressing, mutual masturbation, inter-femoral intercourse, and oral sex are more usual patterns of behaviour. Heterosexual congress, which irresistibly sees itself as directed to penetrative intercourse and thwarted without it, is what prompts the misconception that male homosexuality must be geared to an analogous mode of gratification. It also influences popular ideas of lesbianism, still haunted by the ludicrous myth of the dildo.) Anal intercourse is not unknown as a type of heterosexual intercourse. Heterosexual anal intercourse may be low as a percentage of total copulations, but, having regard to the greater frequency of heterosexual over homosexual sex acts in the population taken as a whole, it may be comparable to homosexual anal intercourse in terms of number of acts. If the Baker hypothesis were correct, one would anticipate that even the initial patterns of HIV spread should show roughly equal proportions of heterosexually and homosexually transmitted infections. The fact that the pattern follows that of other venereal diseases argues the irrelevance of mode of (penetrative) intercourse.

It is often thought that British society, admittedly intolerant of homosexuality in the past, has now become liberal. There is not much truth in this. The legal reforms based on the Wolfenden Report served only to 'decriminalise' some male homosexual acts and greatly increased the penalties for some voluntary sexual acts. This legislation introduced a male homosexual age of consent of 21, as compared to 16 for sexual acts where the participants are a male and a female, and as compared to no statutory restriction where both are female.[8] In the years following these 'liberal' reforms the annual numbers of men punished for consensual homosexual acts has increased (by about three times) and the prison sentences imposed are longer.[9] With the escalating level of public discourse on homosexuality came a more alert scrutiny of those seeking employment, particularly public employment.[10] In England, anyone who has acted as a referee for applicants to the Higher Civil Service, and who has answered questions as part of a 'positive vetting' procedure, will know the extent to which such investigations are directed towards uncovering clues as to possible homosexual experience of applicants. Long-term relationships will tend to be socially visible. Legal and social sanctions against same-sex couples render fidelity to one person more difficult. Males are sexually active well before the age of 21, and by that age may be habituated to the anonymous sexual encounters that institutionalised discrimination facilitates and requires. Mutual abiding love needs no recommendation, but not everyone will find it, and those who do not are unlikely to live in sexual abstinence. Venereal disease control requires the unfrightened co-operation of the citizenry at large. It is undesirable that co-operation should be coerced, and probably a mistake to imagine that it could be. It can be forthcoming where there is equal respect for citizens and equal protection of the law. The requirement of equal protection is increasingly marginalised as a 'gay demand', when it ought to recommend itself impartially to liberal opinion. Equity requires that criminal law should be reformed after the manner of the Napoleonic Code in which laws regarding consent, assault, public decency, and so on, are formulated without regard to the homosexual/heterosexual distinction. Legal systems based on the Napoleonic Code take no cognisance of those categories. In addition, existing legislation against discrimination in employment, housing, and so forth, protecting race, gender, and national origin, should be amended to include as a protected category 'sexual orientation or preference'. It is a cause for dismay, and a thing ominous in itself and for what it implies for the checking of AIDS, that liberal opinion should presently give every appearance of having been frightened to death.

If AIDS in Western countries is arrested at its present state of spread the prejudicial perception of the disease as an essentially homosexual-related phenomenon will be reinforced. If AIDS spreads more extensively via heterosexual activity, as there is reason to anticipate that it will, then one can hope for the doleful consolation that 'discrimination will cease to be an issue once it is seen that the virus itself does not discriminate'.[11] I think that unlikely. Intolerance needs no reasons, only excuses. The more the crops fail, the more the sorcerers will be burned. For this reason it is worth remembering why the sexual authoritarian's hope of a homosexuality-free world is destined to remain unrealised.

Kinsey presents strong evidence for the view that there are no homosexual people, just homosexual acts. Roughly, his position is that homosexuality is a natural phenomenon, but homosexuals are not a natural kind. The expression 'homosexual' does not locate a category of people manifesting a syndrome of characteristic psychological or physiological properties. It is no more an 'essentialist' concept than, say, 'British citizen' or 'Conservative voter'.

> Males do not represent two discrete populations, heterosexual and homosexual. The world is not to be divided into sheep and goats. Not all things are black nor all things white. It is a fundamental of taxonomy that nature rarely deals with discrete categories. Only the human mind invents categories and tries to force facts into separate pigeon-holes. The living world is a continuum in each and every one of its aspects. The sooner we learn this concerning human sexual behaviour the sooner we shall reach a sound understanding of the realities of sex.[12]

Strange as it seems when listening to their representatives, sympathisers and adherents of the 'religious right', the 'moral majority', the Festival of Light, the Conservative party, and the law enforcement agencies, are, taken as groups, found on investigation to have sexual behaviour patterns not significantly different from those found in the larger population:

> The police force and court officials who attempt to enforce the sex laws, the clergymen and business men and every other group in the city which periodically calls for enforcement of the laws – particularly the laws against sexual 'perversion' – have given a record of incidences and frequencies in the homosexual which are as high as those of the rest of the social level to which they belong. It is not a matter of individual hypocrisy which leads officials with homosexual histories to become prosecutors of the homosexual activity in the community. They themselves are the victims of the mores, and the public demand that they protect those mores. As long as there are such gaps between the traditional custom and the actual behaviour of the population, such inconsistencies will continue to exist.[13]

This is not the place to enter into the psychology of it, but, for whatever reasons, 'homophobia', like anti-semitism, is ultimately murderous in its intentions. However, though the genocide of the Jews may be possible, that of 'the homosexuals' is not. Kinsey spells it out in the mordant last paragraph of Chapter 21:

> If all persons with any trace of homosexual history, or those who were predominantly homosexual, were eliminated from the population today, there is no reason for believing that the incidence of the homosexual in the next generation would be materially reduced. The homosexual has been a significant part of human sexual activity ever since the dawn of history, primarily because it is an expression of capacities that are basic in the human animal.[14]

If that is correct, then liberalism is not an escapable option; though I have no doubt that we will exhaust ourselves continuing to escape it.

Notes

1.   Britain's health ministers put out some advertisements on AIDS, but could not bring themselves to use the expression 'anal intercourse'. They mystified or amused the public with 'rectal intercourse' instead. The claims about cervical cancer and its high mortality figure worldwide were taken from a BBC 'Medicine Now' programme.

2.   Doctors have found evidence that a huge belt of Africa, stretching from Zaire to Rwanda, Burundi, Uganda, Tanzania, Kenya, and Zambia, is afflicted with an astonishingly high incidence of AIDS. The statistics quite dwarf European and American figures. In the cities of Zaire, for instance, it is thought that one in ten people carry the AIDS virus. In Kinshasa, the capital, it was reported that there were 2,000 cases of AIDS in city hospitals by the beginning of 1985, and that this figure was rising. In another study, in Uganda, it was revealed that 20 per cent of tested citizens were found to be carriers. In every study, men and women were affected in roughly equal numbers . . . (Robin McKie, *Panic, The Story of AIDS* (with foreword by Anthony Pinching) p. 82, Thorsons Publishing Group, 1986).

'. . . the virus responsible is HTLV3/LAV, the same one that has affected the West. And in all the studies it was found that men and women are affected in equal numbers' (McKie, *Panic*, p. 85). The *Observer* (3 August 1986) reported the compulsory screening of all US army recruits; 261 000 men and 42 000 women were tested, mostly in the age group 18 to 25. Applicants from the New York metropolitan area gave six in every 1000 women as HIV-positive and eight of every 1000 men. The survey found that the ratio of infected males to females overall was 2.5:1 and not the 13:1 extrapolated from earlier figures.

3.   *Guardian*, 27 July 87.

4.   BBC Radio News, 11 Sept. 87. The phrase subsequently used in Section 28 of the Local Government Act 1988 was (that a Local Authority should not) 'promote the teaching in any maintained school of the acceptability of homosexuality as a pretended family relationship'. The Department of Education further explained in a Circular 12/88 that 'Section 28 does not affect the activities of school governors nor of teachers. It will not prevent the objective discussion of homosexuality in the classroom, nor the counselling of pupils concerned about their sexuality'.

5.   McKie (Panic, p. 101) quotes Dr Angus Dalgleish (Institute of Cancer Research, London) as saying:

> I have seen so many cases of men who have contracted AIDS and who insist they could only have got it from prostitutes. I can see no reason why these men should lie. They have developed an extremely

serious condition. There is nothing to be gained in denying homosexual relations they might have had. Yet they insist that they have had none. I think the inference is clear – this is a straightforward sexually transmitted disease.

McKie also points out that:

> One important factor that will have delayed the onset of the disease among heterosexuals is the make-up of the original risk groups. By accident, they are mostly men – male homosexuals; haemophiliacs, who are almost always male; and drug takers, who are predominantly male. That has distorted statistics in a particularly interesting way. If most of the first AIDS victims and virus carriers are male then there can be very few female victims and carriers who can then infect men heterosexually. Because there are a lot more males with the virus, there will be a lot more women picking up the virus from them compared with the number of women who can give the virus to men. And this is exactly what you find. Of the 52 heterosexually infected AIDS victims in New York, fifty were women, and two were men. (*Panic*, p. 103)

6. This point is of particular importance considering the recent rash claims in British newspapers that it is more 'difficult' to contract HIV heterosexually, the implication of these stories being that the mechanisms of vaginal intercourse somehow reduce susceptibility.

7. See Gordon Westwood, *A Minority, A Report on the Life of the Male Homosexual in Great Britain*, ch. 7 (London: Longman, 1960). Eustace Chesser, *Live and Let Live* (London: William Heinemann, 1958) opines:

> From my own clinical experience I doubt if more than 15 per cent of homosexuals are sodomists and I believe that most psychologists would confirm this. What tends to be overlooked is that in heterosexual marriage the practice, or the desire to practise sodomy is probably more than 15 per cent. In an investigation which I carried out in a provincial town many years ago, this practice was accepted by many wives as an insurance against the possibility of pregnancy.

8. This is the most striking of the legal inequalities between male and female in Britain, and the one most obviously having dire consequences for those subject to it. I have never heard a debate on equality of the sexes that mentions the matter.

9. At his second trial Oscar Wilde was convicted of acts of 'gross indecency' with males (some were under 21), and was given the maximum sentence of two years' imprisonment. The trial judge expressed a regret that he was not able to impose a longer sentence. Under the Wolfenden reforms he would be able to do so (six years, in fact). The Wilde case is often cited as an example of something that could not happen nowadays.

10. Increasing quantity of discourse on sexual matters is sometimes misperceived as a rising tide of liberalism. A mistake, as Foucault teaches. (See Michel Foucault, *A History of Sexuality*, vols. 1, 2 and 3).

11. As Brenda Almond succinctly puts it ('Report from the Third International Conference on AIDS', *Times Higher Education Supplement*, 3 July 87).

12. Kinsey, Pomeroy, and Martin, *Sexual Behavior in the Human Male*, p. 639 (W. B. Saunders Co., 1948). I do not hold with the disparagement of Kinsey's work which is sometimes heard. For a defence of its merits, see Stephen Jay Gould, 'Of Wasps and WASPs', in Gould, *The Flamingo's Smile, Reflections in Natural History* (New York: W. W. Norton, 1985, Harmondsworth: Pelican 1985) and, in particular, Wardell B. Pomeroy's splendid book, *Dr. Kinsey and the Institute for Sex Research* (New York: Harper & Row, and New York: Signet Books 1972).

13. Kinsey *et al.*, *Sexual Behavior*, p. 665.

14. Ibid., p. 666.

9 The Legal Implications of AIDS and HIV Infection in Britain and the United States
Alistair Orr

INTRODUCTION

Acquired Immune Deficiency Syndrome was first recognised in the summer of 1981. The virus which may progress to full-blown AIDS was discovered in 1983. Originally this virus had several names but it is now internationally known as the human immunodeficiency virus (HIV).[1] By the end of 1988, it was estimated that between one and one and a half million people had the virus in the United States[2] and up to 50 000 in the United Kingdom.[3] Considering the comparatively short period of time involved, the extent of the disease and the speed with which it has spread is shockingly apparent. The newness and vastness of this 'global pandemic' has raised many issues, not only in the scientific and medical communities, but also at a legal and social level.

CONSTITUTIONAL ISSUES

Arguably the greatest challenge which the law faces with regard to the AIDS epidemic is the reconciliation of the dilemma between the private right of the individual to conduct his or her own life with the public right to health. If AIDS is to be tackled, those who have the virus and those most at risk must be able to seek what treatment is available and provide the health services with information not only about the spread of the disease but also about its very nature. Against this there is the public need to restrict conduct which is likely to spread the disease. Often this is conduct which many find morally offensive, and yet which many others would argue was their right to enjoy. A balance must be struck in order that those at risk are willing to come forward, and that the disease can be treated – otherwise there is a genuine fear that the disease will be driven underground.

Those who have found themselves to have the virus or even to have been at risk of the virus have been subjected to all kinds of discrimination on both sides of the Atlantic. For example, this has occurred in education,[4] employment,[5] housing,[6] and insurance.[7] While these areas will be discussed later, an indication of the kind of difficulties that can arise may be seen in the case of just one such issue: that of refusal of treatment. The United States private health care system is open to different pressures from those exerted upon the British public health care system, but a nursing home in New York has been enjoined from accepting AIDS patients by a group of neighbouring residents,[8] and in Los Angeles two paramedics who allegedly did not provide prompt medical assistance to the victim of a heart attack – in both cases because of a fear of AIDS – were sued.[9]

In the United Kingdom, on the other hand, the Royal College of Nursing has warned that those nurses who refuse to care for AIDS patients face disciplinary action for unprofessional conduct.[10] Although there have been calls for doctors to follow suit,[11] nothing has been done as yet. It has been pointed out that there is a very strong ethical obligation on doctors to treat AIDS patients and if a doctor's refusal to treat such a patient is based on the notion that the illness resulted from voluntary conduct of which the doctor disapproves, then he leaves himself open to a charge of serious professional misconduct before the General Medical Council.[12] While doctors do, reasonably, have fears about contracting the disease, precautions can reduce such a risk to a minimum[13] and some would argue that there should be a special onus on the medical profession to act in a manner which allays public fears and misapprehensions, in order to combat the hysteria which AIDS too easily arouses.

The issue of a right to treatment does point towards the difficulties that must be resolved by the law concerning this disease. Firstly, recognition must be given to the fact that the public are apprehensive of this mysterious and potentially lethal disease, and that they wish to be given some sort of legal protection against it. Secondly, and against this, those who have the disease and – of equal importance – those who are seen as being at risk of contracting the disease must not be unduly restricted or imposed upon by society as a whole, and any restrictions which are placed upon them must be equitable. Essentially what is at issue here is a matter of constitutional law; because of the way in which the American and British legal systems have developed they have different approaches to tackle this.

The American Position

In the United States it is possible, under the Constitution and Bill of Rights, for the Supreme Court to challenge any laws as violating the rights of individuals to, say, liberty, privacy or property.[14] What the courts are increasingly forced to do is to balance rights issues. Different individual rights have independent positive weights and weights of different value[15] and assessing what these are has become firmly entrenched in constitutional decision making. The case of *New York State Association for Retarded Children* v. *Carey*[16] is a relevant example of how this is done. It held that mentally retarded pupils who were carriers of Hepatitis B should not be put in separate classrooms, because the 'relevant inquiry' here was whether on balance the proposed segregation, with its resultant educational disadvantages, would be justified to protect the health and welfare of the non-carrier children. In the circumstances, the health risk was not sufficient to outweigh the burden on individual rights. Civil liberties, then, need not always yield to health risks, but it is too early to say how the courts will react to AIDS. What can be said is that some states have introduced laws demanding the reporting of all AIDS cases, some of positive HIV test results; some have passed legislation closing down places that permitted high-risk activity; and some have modified their laws to allow measures to be taken against those persons who expose others to a risk of infection.[17]

Are the current protections sufficient? In particular, male homosexuals (the group most seriously affected by the disease at present) feel that an epidemic of discrimination is accompanying the epidemic of the disease, and lawyers have noted that this discrimination is driving people with AIDS underground.[18] It is even argued that for gay men 'the Constitution and Bill of Rights offer as little protection . . . as their lost physical immunity'.[19] To counter this, Los Angeles has passed an 'AIDS Discrimination Ordinance',[20] which prohibits discrimination against those with AIDS or HIV infection, and those perceived to be at risk of AIDS in employment, rental housing, business establishments, city facilities and services and educational institutions'. Specific exceptions are made for blood or sperm banks, surrogate mother facilities and other establishments engaged in the exchange of products containing elements of blood and semen. As well as providing the aggrieved person with a means of raising a civil action for damages, costs and punitive damages, the Ordinance can be used by way of injunction (that is, a court order prohibiting a particular act either before it occurs or while it is taking place). This is especially useful to someone with AIDS or HIV, as the prospect of monetary relief after a prolonged court battle could prove pointless for such a person, and the availability of this remedy greatly increases his or her power over the person who is exercising discrimination. A caveat has been placed on the ambit of the Ordinance, namely that religious organisations and conduct which is necessary to protect the health and safety of the general public are exempted from coverage. If one wishes to rely on this one has to prove, firstly, that the discrimination was a 'necessary result of a necessary course of conduct', and, secondly, that no less discriminating means of protection exists.

While this local statute does provide a protection against discrimination it is also to be applauded for the role that it takes in trying to educate the public about the AIDS virus.[21] It is, however, very much a unique phenomenon, and the protection which it offers is not available in most parts of the United States.

The British Position

The British constitutional position is significantly different. Fundamentally there is no written constitution and no bill of rights. Discrimination has been addressed at a legislative level with regard to both sex and race,[22] but little has been done outside that. In particular, again with regard to male homosexuals, very little has been done to ease discrimination against them (although homosexual activity between consenting adults has been decriminalised following the Wolfenden Report).[23] In Britain, then, it would be very difficult to prove that one had been subjected to unfair treatment through being seen as at risk of contracting AIDS or HIV (although it may be possible to rely on other legislation, for example, prohibiting unfair dismissal from employment).

Certain laws have been passed in the United Kingdom which do have reference to the HIV infection. The Public Health (Infectious Diseases) Regulations 1985[24] did not make AIDS a notifiable disease, largely on the grounds that the disease is not particularly infectious and to do so would have put unacceptable restrictions on sufferers,[25] which is very important when it is desired not to drive them underground. On the other hand, the Public Health (Control of Diseases) Act 1984 allows, in 'exceptional circumstances', for orders to be made so that patients believed to have AIDS may be compulsorily examined and for AIDS patients to be removed to hospital and detained. How far this can go is a matter of uncertainty, but great weight appears to be attached to the need for the circumstances to be exceptional; it is claimed that there has been only one case where it has been necessary to remove someone compulsorily to hospital under the Act.[26]

CONFIDENTIALITY

Another aspect of this subject, and one which has a certain relevance to constitutional issues, is that of confidentiality. There is a genuine worry that if those who are at risk of the disease and those who actually have contracted the disease are not protected by a legal obligation demanding confidentiality then they will be slow to come forward and more people may be put at risk. The Hippocratic oath imposes confidentiality on the doctor in all his dealings with patients. As has already been noted, there are situations in which the interest of the individual may be overtaken by the public interest. What protection, then, should there be for the individual at risk so that he will not be deterred from seeking medical help, and when does the public interest become sufficiently important to override this?

In the United States, the right of privacy is not explicit in the Constitution, but a right to privacy has been held to exist in certain medical matters.[27] Further, state constitutions and laws may provide protection against the invasion of privacy, although statutes have also been passed requiring doctors to inform the relevant authorities that a patient has a communicable disease. When the information is passed on to these authorities there is a risk of the information falling into the hands of third parties, such as insurance companies.

Illinois, California and Wisconsin have all adopted specific legislation safeguarding the confidentiality of individuals who are tested for the presence of the AIDS virus at blood banks and alternative test sites. Wisconsin, California and Florida prohibit the use of the test result to determine eligibility for disability, health or life insurance or to terminate employment. Particularly regarding test results there is a very strong argument for saying that this information should only be disclosed once a written consent has been given.[28]

In the United Kingdom, it has been recognised that the doctor's duty to respect patient's confidentiality is not absolute, and that a doctor can be ordered by the courts to breach confidentiality.[29] But what of the situation where the courts are not involved, and a doctor feels entitled or perhaps even obliged to disclose information regarding one of his patients? The General Medical Council has outlined a number of guidelines concerning the disclosure of confidential information.[30] One of these grounds is where the 'public interest' demands that the doctor's duty to maintain confidentiality should be overridden. It has been emphasised that this is not limited to crimes alone.[31] The doctor should, though, first endeavour to persuade the patient if he is going to tell another and do his utmost to obtain that patient's consent. But the doctor must also balance against his patient's interest the risk to other individuals. When the doctor reasonably foresees that non-disclosure poses a real risk of harm to a third party then he should be free to warn that third party, especially if that person is also his patient. Similarly, if a doctor thought it more appropriate, he could contact the doctor of the third party. This would permit a doctor to tell the sexual partner or partners of someone with the disease about this patient's condition, provided he had first sought the approval of the patient and this had been refused.[32] In keeping with this, the National Health Service (Venereal Diseases) Regulations 1974 make specific exceptions to the duty on health authorities to ensure that the identity of a sexually-transmitted disease sufferer is kept confidential.[33] Exceptions apply in those cases in which revealing the identity of the sufferer to someone will enable that person to be treated or where it will prevent the disease from spreading to others. It is thought that even where HIV is not contracted as a result of sex similar grounds could apply.[34]

The leading British case on this, *X v. Y*[35], concerned a slightly different aspect of the confidentiality issue. Here a newspaper was prevented from publishing a list of people with AIDS which included two medical practitioners. It held that the public interest in preserving the confidentiality of hospital records identifying people with AIDS outweighed the public interest in the freedom of the press to publish such information. It was argued that those with the disease should not be deterred from going to hospital because of fear of discovery, and also that an informed debate about the disease could take place without publication of this confidential information.

In conclusion, it may be said that confidentiality must be respected if the doctor is to maintain the trust of his patient, but that there is a limit on this confidentiality when it is putting others at severe risk. Only those people, though, who are in this high-risk category need be told, and others, such as even the family and friends of a sufferer, far less their employers or insurers, should not be informed. An exception must also be made for research into AIDS and the virus. Here, however, protection for patients might well be needed.[36]

TESTING

One of the areas in which the issue of confidentiality is of fundamental importance is that of testing for the presence of the AIDS virus. At present testing is generally done on the basis of discovering whether there are antibodies to HIV present in a person's blood. Such tests do not determine the level of infection with the virus, nor do they show that a person has AIDS, nor even that a person is going to develop AIDS. It must also be pointed out that results can be 'false positives' (declaring someone to be seropositive when they are not) or 'false negatives' (declaring someone not to be seropositive when they are), and that there is a certain latency period between acquiring the virus and testing positively (which varies, but may be as much as three months). Testing has been advocated in a number of different ways, which will be considered in turn.

Mandatory Testing

While, at first sight, universal mandatory testing might seem to offer a solution, there are a number of significant difficulties which invalidate it. Among these must be the issue of cost, especially where that is allied to the points which have already been made. It would seem, too, that if the exercise were to be useful, people would have to be tested regularly. Additionally, it has been estimated[37] that, in spite of a high level of accuracy, the generally low rate of infection in the population as a whole would result in a considerable number of false positives. Consequently more sophisticated and expensive tests would have to be offered to everyone who had tested positively, as they already are in the case of voluntary testing. More importantly, to test everyone without their consent presents a significant challenge to individual liberty. Such a challenge could perhaps be justified if therapeutic intervention was available or others were put at risk by social contact,[38] but in the absence of both of these it makes a significant encroachment on personal freedom. There is also little hope, given the vastness of such an enterprise, that it would succeed in combating the spread of AIDS.

Mandatory testing or screening of special groups is a different matter. Again respect needs to be paid to individual rights and one must ask if there are sufficient justifications for overriding them. In most instances, such as education, most employment and certain insurance matters there are not these justifications, but in certain instances they may exist. For example, although it would be unnecessary to test all those who are in hospital, it may be worthwhile to test patients in certain areas because of the dangers of transmission, say, in dialysis units. Also there are factors peculiar to the prison environment which may mean that testing is acceptable.[39]

One measure which has aroused controversy is the American decision to test all immigrants for the virus. Applicants can, under existing American law,[40] be denied visas if they are afflicted with any 'dangerous contagious diseases', and steps have been taken to include the AIDS virus within that category.[41]

Voluntary Testing

Voluntary testing arouses the least objection, as those to be tested have taken the initiative themselves. The test is 'not just another test'[42] and before anyone is tested they must be fully counselled regarding the nature and limits of the test, the consequences of a positive result and the consequences of a negative result. Following on from this, it is argued that, if one can avoid the test because of its potential harm, then one should do so, provided one behaves in a responsible fashion as if one had the virus. There is even talk of a 'right to ignorance'. It is understandable that those who belong to risk groups are wary of taking the test, but, provided those who test positively are guaranteed a reasonable level of confidentiality and provided steps are taken to minimise discrimination, it is better that they come forward for advice and treatment. Being able to treat AIDS and HIV may well depend on being able to monitor it, and no accurate overall picture of the disease can be built up if significant numbers of those with the virus remain 'hidden'.

Allied to the notion of voluntary testing is that of the issuing of AIDS-free cards. According to those who favour such an idea, it would provide people with a non-legal impetus to be tested and, although it has limits, it would be an effective means of limiting the spread of the disease.[43] But there are several severe limitations on such a scheme: there are practical problems in screening; the cards can create an illusion of safety; and confidentiality is an important issue which the use of cards might subvert.[44] Perhaps the best argument against the use of such a card is the fact that it is 'spent' after one sexual encounter and so they are hardly worth the paper they are printed on!

Testing without Consent

Many doctors have felt, understandably, that they are in danger of contracting the virus and have accordingly advocated the need for testing certain patients, sometimes without the patient's consent. Their justification for this is that performing such an act can be upsetting to the patient, to say nothing of the devastation that a positive result may bring. But while one must appreciate the fears of doctors, one must not lose sight of the interest of patients.

The law confers on everyone a right to determine what is done to his body, and if that person's body is invaded by being intentionally touched by another against that person's will then a battery has been committed. In medical matters, the courts have been reluctant to hold a doctor liable in battery where a general consent to the touching has taken place.[45] However, where the touching has been considerably different from that to which consent has been given, then the courts have been willing to classify this as a battery, even where the treatment that took place as a result of the touching could reasonably be said to be in the interests of the patient.[46] When a doctor takes a blood sample from a patient he is legally 'touching' the patient, and so the patient's consent should be sought.

If anyone is treated without giving express consent, for a disease for which there is no cure and, if he tests positively, which could result in him having to make significant changes in his life-style, then this could be argued to be against the interests of the patient. Accordingly the patient must be told about the implications of this blood testing before he gives consent, since if this information is not given the patient will be able to raise an action for battery against the doctor with a reasonable chance of success. Much has been made of the fact that testing has always been done without doctors seeking consent, but the AIDS virus and the consequences of being found seropositive are significant enough to merit express consent from all patients before they can be tested, as this testing cannot be readily compared with testing for other medical conditions.

One legal opinion spelt out the differences.[47] Firstly, there is no vaccine, no primary treatment and no cure for the condition. Secondly, while the diagnosis of any serious condition carries trauma this is increased by the unique stigma attached to AIDS and HIV so that many patients prefer not to know whether they are infected. Thirdly, public authorities currently assure the public that no testing will be performed without full consent. Fourthly, it has been argued that testing for the virus can affect insurance applications whether or not the result is positive. It should be noted that these reasons were all given to warn doctors that they might leave themselves open to a claim in negligence (which requires proof of fault) if they were to test patients without consent. However there is no reason why they could not be marshalled to the patient's cause in the battery action, especially when they are allied to the arguments that testing is only a research procedure (and a non-therapeutic one at that) and that the doctor can simply treat the patient as infected if that patient declines the test.

A patient who wished to suggest that he had been wronged in this way could possibly raise both battery and negligence actions. One potential limit on the latter course could be the difficulty of proving that a tangible injury had resulted (which is unnecessary in a battery action).

Considerable discussion has surrounded the issue of testing without consent in the United Kingdom, particularly at recent meetings of the British Medical Association. Counsel's opinion has stated that patients should be told if they are to be tested for HIV, and they should agree to the testing.[48] If they do not then they should be treated as if they are infected. Any doctor who tests patients without consent must be prepared to defend that position before the courts or the General Medical Council.

The American Medical Association has voted against the mandatory testing of those groups at high risk of infection with HIV – instead doctors should encourage those at risk to take the test.[49]

Anonymous Testing

Finally, a mention should be made of anonymous testing. This again is done without the explicit consent of the patient. The patient does not learn the result of the test, and the doctor who tests the blood does not know the identity of the patient, but only the age, sex and location of the patient whose sample is tested. A general consent is given by the patient to the removal of the blood and its testing for other purposes, and the patient can normally voice an objection to the blood being tested for the virus. The rationale behind such a measure is to try to build up a picture of the way in which the disease is spreading and, from that, to develop strategies to check that spread.

Such testing has been permitted in the United States for some time, but it has only recently been allowed in Britain.[50] This has been because a number of moral or ethical problems were recognised, rather than any great legal hurdles.[51] Because the patient is not forced to confront a potential HIV antibody status without personally submitting to the test, and because there would be tremendous difficulties in proving loss or damages, there is little chance of a successful action in tort. Further, such studies as have been done suggest that this minimal infringement of individual rights may well be of public benefit in predicting the spread of the virus.[52]

CRIMINAL LAW

Another area of the law on which the disease has already had some impact is that of the criminal law, and this looks likely to increase in the future. Unfortunately, in those situations where the law has stepped in and where it is being urged to step in, little thought has been given to the possible consequences.

For example, in the United States there have been calls by doctors that criminal sanctions, where they do not already exist, should be reintroduced against homosexuals.[53] Stricter enforcement of existing criminal law has also been advocated, so that laws against prostitution, laws against commercialised sex and prohibitions on 'sex-facilitating emporia' should all be rigorously enforced.[54] Such 'vindictive' legislation begins to confuse morality and criminal law, and can only serve to make it overwhelmingly difficult for those who are seropositive to come forward. Others have argued that the role of the criminal law in the AIDS crisis should only be a minor one[55] – in areas such as prohibition, prostitution, pornography and drug use the criminal law does not really manage to change behaviour and the existence of too strict laws can be damaging to respect for the law and legal institutions. Indeed the AIDS epidemic may cause society to consider with greater honesty issues which have previously been clouded in dishonesty, prejudice and discrimination, especially in the areas of sexuality and drug taking.

Apart from these initiatives in the criminal law, sanctions may apply against people who knowingly transfer the virus to another, or who knowingly put others at risk through having sexual intercourse with them. While reference must be made to this, it is highly dubious whether the criminal law can be used as a means of preventing the spread of the disease. To start with, its effect in genuinely deterring conduct in sexual matters is limited (in prostitution, for example) and it only comes into play after the damage has been done. Education is at least as effective and comes into play before the damage has occurred.

In the United States it may well be possible to argue that passing on the virus might be homicide, or attempted murder, or criminal assault.[56] Yet all of these present a number of difficulties if they are to be fitted within the existing legal framework; if it is desired to make such conduct criminal, it may be better to consider legislation.

In the United Kingdom, the criminal law of Scotland diverges from the criminal law of England and Wales. For the latter, the leading authority is that of *R. v. Clarence*,[57] which held that a man who passed on gonorrhoea to his wife was not guilty of assault. This highly criticised decision was based on a prosecution under S.20 or S.47 of the Offences Against the Person Act 1861. It does not exclude the possibility of a prosecution under S.23 of the Act which prohibits maliciously administering any poison or other destructive and noxious thing – using this may be the best means of seeking a conviction.[58] The 1861 Act does not apply in Scotland, but there it has long been recognised that '[a]ll intentional infliction of physical injury is criminal'.[59] Authority for this comes from a definition of common law assault made in the eighteenth century which was relied on in a recent decision that held the sale of 'glue sniffing kits' to children to be criminal.[60] Following this, it would be possible to prosecute someone for assault by alleging that they had wilfully and recklessly infected others with the virus by sexual intercourse. In spite of all this, it may well prove impossible to show in court that a particular person transferred the virus to another, given the latency period of the virus and the possibility of other contacts.

As a footnote to this discussion it is worth noting that the AIDS virus may well prove to have an impact on other areas of criminal law. For example, a man who killed his sexual partner after the latter admitted he had AIDS tried to use this as a 'heat of passion' defence.[61] Also fear of the disease has been used as a 'defence'[62] and it has been suggested that certain offences, such as rape, might be aggravated by it.[63] How the law will react to these developments will depend on the circumstances of the different cases.

TORT LAW

The tort law of negligence provides the individual with a system of compensation where he or she is wronged by another, and where that person could be regarded as having a duty of care to that individual. Unfortunately, with reference to the AIDS virus, the law of tort suffers from many of the same limitations previously noted about the criminal law. There are a number of different heads under which a tort action for sexual transmission of the virus could be raised[64] but the most significant are those of negligence or battery.

If one is to succeed in a negligence action then one must prove three things. Firstly, there needs to be a legal duty owed by the defendant to the plaintiff, which must have been breached. However, the exact legal standing of sexual partners – particularly if they are not married – is very uncertain, and so it might be difficult to prove that a legal duty existed. This at least is the traditional position, although recent litigation in the United States has held that such a legal duty does exist.[65] Secondly, there needs to be a causal connection between the act or omission complained about and any resulting damages claimed. Given that there could well be other sexual contacts before symptoms manifest themselves, proving this could be almost impossible. And thirdly, there must have been damages or loss resulting from the breach of duty. Here questions of contributory negligence and voluntary assumption of risk can be raised, together with any time restrictions that may be imposed on raising an action under the legal doctrine of limitation. One can readily appreciate, therefore, that the chances of success in such actions are likely to be very low indeed.

A battery action could circumvent many of these difficulties, but in order to show the requisite intention for this 'unlawful touching' it would probably be necessary to show that the defendant knew about his or her infectious condition and this could be awkward to prove.

Additionally, as with criminal law, punishment or compensation is scant redress for those who have acquired a potentially lethal condition. Particularly in the civil action there is a danger, given the protracted nature of such legal proceedings and the length of time that the condition takes to manifest itself, that either the victim or the culprit will have died and so little beneficial vindication will be secured.

In America there has also arisen the question of whether liability could be attached to any party where blood products transmit the AIDS virus or other similar diseases.[66] But as nearly all jurisdictions have taken the opinion that the supply of blood is a service and not a product, and hence success in claiming must meet the rigours of proving fault rather than being able to rely on strict product liability, one's chances of success in such an action are very slim.

Speculation has surrounded the American decision of *Tarasoff* v. *Regents of the University of California*[67] concerning the professional's 'duty to warn' third parties where they are placed at risk by the patient. In this case a psychiatrist was held to have a duty to warn a woman that his patient was contemplating killing her. It is still unclear how American courts will deal with the issue of liability for failure to inform a third party of a patient's antibody positive status.

DEBILITATING EFFECTS OF THE VIRUS

One area which has received little legal attention thus far, perhaps because if offers limited potential for litigation, is that of how the person with AIDS continues to look after his affairs as the disease affects him more severely. Unfortunate though this may be for the individual concerned, this has opened up a 'new market' for the lawyer – not only in the control of the patient's financial matters, but also in directing the patient's medical management.[68]

Several factors contribute to this situation. Significantly the AIDS sufferer is likely to be comparatively young and may well not have considered how to distribute whatever estate he has at the time of his death. If he is a homosexual then it is necessary for him to make every effort to write a will and declare expressly whom he wishes to receive his estate, otherwise his natural family will receive it all and others close to him might be entirely excluded. Another matter which may well be worth considering for the person with HIV or AIDS is how he can minimise tax liability on his death. To discuss these issues is hardly cheering, but many may feel happier for having organised their affairs responsibly. Additionally the disease is known to affect brain tissue, and while the extent of this is, at present, uncertain, it could mean that people with AIDS can only play a gradually decreasing role in the conduct of their affairs.

Regarding medical matters, there is in California the Durable Power of Attorney for Health Care Act 1984 which allows patients of sound mind to designate others to make their health care decisions for them if they should become incompetent.[69] In the United Kingdom recent cases regarding the mentally handicapped have pointed to the inadequate provisions for the giving of consent to medical treatment when the person is incapable of giving that consent personally.[70] There have been calls for substantial reforms of the law.[71] At present, people would be well advised to talk matters through with their doctors and inform them in advance, perhaps even in writing, as to how they would like to be treated.

A brief mention may be made here of euthanasia. Courts in the United States and the United Kingdom have been reluctant to punish 'mercy killings' severely, but these acts are still illegal in both jurisdictions.[72] It is now generally recognised that suicide and attempted suicide are not crimes, but that assisting a person to commit suicide is still criminal.[73] The law seems to reflect the approach advocated by Philippa Foot – that in some individual cases euthanasia is *morally* acceptable, but that it should not be legalised because of the problems of abuse.[74]

SOME AREAS OF SPECIAL RELEVANCE

Emphasis has been placed on the need for the law to protect those with the virus and those at most risk, and also on the public need to minimise the spread of the disease. Conflicts between these two values have meant that certain particular areas and categories of persons are worthy of special comment. It is worthwhile here to make some remarks on a few of these special areas and groups.

Employment

Testing a workforce can arouse strong ethical objections,[75] but it may be justified in economic terms. In the United States the issue of employment discrimination against those seen as being at risk of AIDS or HIV had hinged on the issue of whether AIDS can be classified as a 'handicap' or 'disability' under federal law,[76] and, in particular, whether it comes within the terms of the Rehabilitation Act of 1973.[77] One of the first reported cases regarding employment discrimination and the disease was that of *Shuttleworth* v. *Broward County*.[78] It held that the dismissal of an employee because he had AIDS constituted discrimination against a handicapped person, which is unlawful under a Florida statute. More recently the Supreme Court have held that a teacher who suffered from tuberculosis and was dismissed from her job could be considered as handicapped under the 1973 Act and was protected from discrimination.[79] Although the court said that the ruling did not touch the question of whether AIDS would be covered by the Rehabilitation Act, many people now feel that this could provide a legal precedent for it to do just that. It should be noted that the 1973 Act only covers those employed under federal programmes and so its application is limited.

In the United Kingdom AIDS is not a notifiable disease and consequently there is no obligation on an employee to report to his employer that he has the virus or the syndrome. The guide-lines issued by the Department of Employment[80] say that there is no risk to the public where there is no contact with bodily fluids of an infected person, that few jobs involve such contact and that the majority of employees are therefore safe from infection at work. On the other hand, some employers might feel that because AIDS is not a notifiable disease and because their employees are under no general obligation to disclose their antibody status there is sufficient reason for demanding a test.[81] If this latter view is adopted, employers would be well advised to inform their employees in advance that any general medical examination would include testing for the AIDS virus.

There may be types of employment for which those with the virus are unsuited. An example of this is the airline pilot – it is thought that the debilitating effects of the virus may affect a pilot's ability to make 'snap judgments'. Such personnel are already subjected to stringent medical examination. Also health professionals involved in particularly risky activities might be expected to be tested for seropositivity.

Should an employee be dismissed, either because he is perceived as being at risk of AIDS or the virus, or because he has been shown to be HIV-positive, then he may have a claim for unfair dismissal. To counteract this, an employer could either rely on a defence that the employee's sickness and absence from work justified dismissal, or that there was 'other substantial reason' for ending employment.[82] There would be difficulty in upholding the latter defence, unless a group of employees were refusing to work with the particular indi-vidual. In such a case it may be better to refer the matter to a recognised industrial reconciliation procedure.

Limits on testing within employment are not present when an applicant presents himself for a new appointment. One recent case shows that a limited degree of protection may be available under legislation preventing indirect discrimination on the grounds of sex,[83] but there is significantly greater danger of discrimination at this stage rather than in continuing employment, and fewer safeguards to tackle it.

Insurance

The matter of insurance has considerably greater importance in America than it does in Britain, because health insurance schemes are relied upon to meet American hospital fees, whereas British hospitals are publicly funded. When one looks at the heavy costs of caring for the AIDS patient, it appears that, if these people can be successfully excluded by the insurance companies, Medicaid will be forced to shoulder an overwhelming financial burden.[84] At least two states – California and Wisconsin – prohibit insurance companies from requiring applicants to take the antibody test, but, even where this does happen, the insurance companies are using substitutes for these tests or else denying new policies on social grounds. It may be that steps should be taken to prevent discrimination against sufferers where health insurance is concerned,[85] but, given that a level of discrimination is the essence of insurance, it may be difficult to exclude testing from life insurance matters.[86] Efforts should be made to prevent insurance companies from having access to confidential records, and those who are concerned by such developments should be informed of other financial protection they can use.

Children at School

Many parents are very worried by the AIDS virus, and will go to great lengths to prevent their children being exposed to it. Is the risk of classroom contagion sufficient to prevent pupils who have the virus from attending school alongside those not infected? The leading case on this is the American decision of *District 27 Community School Board* v. *Board of Education*,[87] which held that children with AIDS should not automatically be excluded from school. Indeed the overwhelming medical evidence that AIDS was not transmissible in the classroom setting suggested that a policy of excluding all children with AIDS from school would violate federal law on the children's rights to equal protection of the laws. However some local school districts in America have barred entry of children with

AIDS, even in states that have issued guide-lines against exclusion.

In the United Kingdom a similar policy has been adopted;[88] emphasis has been placed on the fact that the benefits of schooling for the child far outweigh any risk of transmission and that those involved in education should be aware of the potential isolation of a child if he is known to be infected. At present this appears to have been successfully implemented in practice.[89]

Another aspect of children at school and the AIDS virus is that society must realise that a number of children of school age do have a number of 'experiments' as part of the adolescent process, most notably in the 'high-risk' areas of sexual activity and the taking of drugs. While every effort should be made by the educational authorities not to encourage this, some pupils will always put themselves at risk, and to protect them adequate education should be given to school children from an early age.

Prisoners

The system of dealing with prisoners with AIDS in British prisons has been described by Dr John Kilgour, the Director of the British Prison Medical Service.[90] On admission each prisoner is asked if he is likely to be in a risk category and, if so, he is asked to undertake a test. Those who test positively are allowed to participate in the normal prison regime, subject to certain sensible restrictions, and the staff with a need to know are told. On this basis there can be largely unrestricted association and exercise without the need for banishment to prison hospital, but AIDS cases are required to occupy either communal cells together or single cells. It should be added that prisoners are entitled to withhold their consent to treatment – which would include being tested for the virus. If a prisoner did this he could be treated as HIV-positive, or if public interest demanded it an application could be made under the Public Health (Control of Disease) Act 1984.[91] Such measures may well prove impractical in preventing the spread of AIDS and HIV in British prisons.

In America the compulsory testing of all prisoners is to be introduced[92] and it is already permissible to segregate prisoners on the basis of whether or not they have the AIDS virus.[93]

Can a policy of interfering with this aspect of individual liberty be justified in prison? It is known that both intravenous drug use and sex, often forced, does occur in prison.[94] Condoms may be introduced to prisons, but they are hardly likely to be used in forced sex, and sterile syringes and needles are even less likely to be freely distributed in prisons. Confinement in prison already represents a substantial reduction in one's freedoms and it is easier to permit testing and segregation in these circumstances. More significantly, society has a special duty to protect those whom it chooses to incarcerate or institutionalise. Nevertheless it should be official policy not to test those who are detained awaiting trial, but only those who have been found guilty. Prisons may prove an important vector in transferring the virus to the heterosexual community, and the United Kingdom may well wish to introduce legislation bringing it more into line with the American position.

Prostitutes and Intravenous Drug-Users

It is often claimed that prostitutes and intravenous drug-users are the means through which AIDS will be heterosexually transmitted to the general public. Recent studies suggest that it is, in fact, intravenous drug use which poses the vastly greater risk.[95] One particular study comparing the 'legalised' prostitutes of Nevada (of whom very few admitted to sharing needles) with a group of prostitutes in prison (who all acknowledged intravenous drug use)[96] showed that, amongst prostitutes, intravenous drug-users are at much higher risk of contracting the virus (despite the Nevada prostitutes having a vastly higher number of sexual contacts). It has already been argued that both prostitution and drug use are likely to continue, whatever the law tries to do about them. It follows that legislation should be directed at prevention of further spread of the virus. Some would argue that the best way to do this would be to decriminalise prostitution and introduce a system of registration,[97] but there seems little prospect of this at present. A more realistic policy, then, would be to encourage prostitutes to accept regular screening for sexually transmitted diseases, at the same time meeting the prostitutes' own expressed wish for more comprehensive health education.

Intravenous drug-users pose more complicated problems. Drug addicts are 'among the most difficult people to educate',[98] and, additionally, many of them will have reconciled themselves to the fact that their habit itself has lethal potential. A worthwhile effort can still be made to help this group,[99] based on a three-pronged approach: firstly, making sterile equipment available; secondly, directing health education at those groups who need it; and thirdly, identifying and treating those who are HIV-positive.

CONCLUSION

The relative novelty of the AIDS phenomenon, coupled with the immensity of its threat, have meant that the law, which is traditionally somewhat slow to adapt itself to new circumstances, has been thrown into an arena where everything is changing very rapidly. Nevertheless three main factors can be discerned as likely to influence the development of the law.

First, there is a need for what the Americans call 'rights balancing' in the assessment of how the law should react to particular issues. The *District 27*[100] and the *X v. Y*[101] decisions are excellent examples of this; the interest of the individual, to have the freedoms which everyone else enjoys, must be realistically balanced against any threat that the individual poses to public health. But the law should be based only on what is scientifically justifiable rather than on unsubstantiated fears and demands for an unattainable level of safety.

Secondly, legal initiatives are, to an enormous extent, the tools of their political masters. As the virus spreads it is likely to gain also in its political impact. There is universal agreement that the way to control the disease is through behavioural modification, but how that modification is to be achieved arouses widespread disagreement. To encourage responsible behaviour by individuals it will be necessary for governments and legal institutions to behave responsibly, and not out of fear and prejudice.

Thirdly, the law is, at best, limited in its ability to tackle the AIDS threat. This will require co-ordinated action, with the establishment of national commissions consisting not only of lawyers but of medical professionals, scientists, sociologists, representatives of affected groups and other interested parties. These commissions would be able not only to advise governments, but also to monitor national efforts, to bring together organisations fighting the disease and to report to the public.

Notes

BMJ	*British Medical Journal*
ABAJ	*American Bar Association Journal*
UCLA LR	*UCLA Law Review*
JAMA	*Journal of American Medical Association*
SI	*Statutory Instrument*
JME	*Journal of Medical Ethics*
All ER	*All England Reports*
Stanford LR	*Stanford Law Review*
SLT	*Scots Law Times*
NLJ	*New Law Journal*
New Eng J Med	*New England Journal of Medicine*
Amer Jour of Public Health	*American Journal of Public Health*
Harvard LR	*Harvard Law Review*
Hofstra LR	*Hofstra Law Review*
Brit J. Hosp Med	*British Journal of Hospital Medicine*

1. Michael W. Adler, 'ABC of AIDS: Development of the Epidemic', 1987, 294 *BMJ*, p. 1083.
2. William L. Heyward and James W. Curran, 'The Epidemiology of AIDS in the US', *Scientific American*, October 1988, p. 52.
3. Thomson Prentice, '17,000 AIDS deaths by 1992', *The Times*, 1 December 1988.
4. For example, the case of Ryan White, who was initially excluded from school but eventually allowed back – to the disagreement of many parents; David M. Freeman, 'Wrong Without Remedy', *ABAJ*, June 1986, p. 36.
5. For example, 'Lawyers' fear of AIDS led to sack', *Guardian*, 9 December 1986.
6. For example, *People of New York* v. *49 West 12 Tenants Corp.* No. 43604/83 (NY Supreme Court, 20 December 1983) reported in G. W. Matthews and V. F. Neslund, 'The Initial Impact of AIDS on Public Health Law in the United States – 1986' (1987) 257 *JAMA*, p. 344. This case held that it was a violation of a New York Human Rights Law to refuse to renew a physician's lease because he treated AIDS patients on the premises.

7. For example, *National Gay Right Advocates* v. *Great Republic Insurance Company* No. 857323 (San Francisco Super. Ct. filed 5 May, 1986) reported in Matthews and Neslund, 'Initial Impact'. Here gay rights activists have filed a $11 million lawsuit contending that the practice of requiring unmarried male applicants to answer special questions is in contravention of the state insurance regulations that prohibit discrimination against homosexuals.

8. 'Queens judge orders New York City not to put AIDS patients in nursing home', *The New York Times*, 1 August 1985.

9. E. Flaherty, 'A Legal Emergency Brewing over AIDS', *National Law Journal*, 9 July 1984, p. 44.

10. Seumas Milne, 'Nurses ordered to care for AIDS victims', *Guardian*, 3 December 1986.

11. Tony Smith, 'Editorial – AIDS: a doctor's duty' (1987) 294 *BMJ*, p. 6.

12. Raanan Gillon, 'Refusal to treat AIDS and HIV-positive patients' (1987) 294 *BMJ*, p. 1332.

13. M. A. Sande, 'Transmission of AIDS. The case against casual contagion', (1986) 314 *New England J. Med.*, p. 380: '. . . caring for AIDS patients even when there is intensive exposure to contaminated secretions, is not a high-risk activity'. D. J. Cotton, 'The Impact of AIDS on the Medical Care System' (1988) 260 *JAMA*, pp. 519–520.

14. Anonymous, 'The Constitutional Rights of AIDS Carriers' (1986) 99 Harvard L. R., p. 1274.

15. See Deborah Jones Merritt, 'The Constitutional Balance between Health and Liberty', in *AIDS: Public Health and Civil Liberties*, A Hastings Center Report Special Supplement (December 1986) p. 2.

16. 466 F. Supp. 487 (1978).

17. For a discussion of this legislation see Matthews and Neslung, 'Initial Impact'.

18. Cheryl Frank, 'AIDS data-sharing: help sought to combat bias' (1986) 72 *ABAJ*, p. 22.

19. Leonard Orland and Sue L. Wise, 'The AIDS Epidemic: A Constitutional Conundrum' (1985) 14 *Hofstra LR*, pp. 137–138.

20. Prohibition Against Discrimination Based on a Person Suffering from the Medical Condition AIDS, or any Medical Signs or Symptoms Related Thereto, or any perception that a Person is Suffering from the Medical Condition AIDS Whether Real or Imaginary, LOS ANGELES, CAL., CODE Ch. 4, art. 5.8 (1985).

21. Robert Roden 'Educating Through the Law: The Los Angeles Discrimination Ordinance' (1986) 33 *UCLA LR*, p. 1410.

22. Harry Street, *Freedom, the Individual and the Law* (Harmondsworth: Penguin, 5th edn, 1982) ch. 13.

23. *Report of the Committee on Homosexual Offences and Prostitution*, Cmnd. 247 (London: HMSO, 1957).

24. S. I. 85/434.

25. R. G. S. Aitken, 'AIDS: Some Myths and Realities', 1987, 84 *Law Society's Gazette*, p. 239.

26. Aitken, 'Myths and Realities'.

27. *Roe* v. *Wade* 410 US 113 (1973) – a right to privacy in making personal

decisions about abortion up to the point of viability.

28. Madeleine M. Weldon-Linne, C. Michael Weldon-Linne and Julie L. Murphy, 'AIDS-Virus Antibody Testing: Issues of Informed Consent and Patient Confidentiality' (1986) 75 *Illinois Bar Journal*, p. 206.
29. *Hunter* v. *Mann* [1974] 1 QB 767 – where a doctor was required to disclose information because of a statutory duty; and *Nuttall* v. *Nuttall and Twyman* (1964) 2 *Lancet* 145 – where a doctor was required to disclose information in an adultery action.
30. These are outlined and discussed by Margaret Brazier in *Medicine, Patients and the Law* (Harmondsworth: Penguin, 1987) pp. 36 ff.
31. Although it may be possible to argue that if the doctor does not disclose information then a crime may well be committed. See below.
32. The British Medical Association ruled in December 1985 that doctors have a right to tell a spouse or lover that their partner has AIDS, even if the patient does not agree to the disclosure: Graham Hancock and Enver Carim, *AIDS: The Deadly Epidemic* (London: Victor Gollancz, 1986) p. 25.
33. S. I. 74/29.
34. Aitken, 'Myths and Realities'.
35. [1988] 2 All ER 649.
36. Joni N. Gray and Gary B. Melton, 'The Law and Ethics of Psychosocial Research on AIDS', 1985, 64 *Nebraska LR*, p. 637.
37. Weldon-Linne *et al.*, 'Informed Consent'.
38. Ronald Bayer, Carol Levine and Susan M. Wolf, 'HIV Antibody Screening: An Ethical Framework for Evaluating Proposed Programs', 1986, 256 *JAMA*, p. 1768.
39. The American armed forces have introduced mandatory testing for all recruits; M. D. Kirby has suggested that the forces can, like prisons, claim to be subject to different rules because both are 'disciplined situations': 'AIDS Legislation – Turning up the Heat?' 1986, 12 *J. Med. Ethics*, p. 187. The legality of screening prisoners in the United Kingdom is dubious – see below.
40. Section 212(a)(6) of the Immigration and Nationality Act (8 USCA. 1182 (West 1970 and Supp. 1986)).
41. Patrick Brogan, 'US Gets Ready to AIDS Test Immigrants and Convicts', *Independent*, 10 June 1987.
42. Miller *et al.*, 'HTLV-III: Should Testing ever be Routine?', 1986, 292 *BMJ*, p. 941.
43. Julian Peto, 'AIDS: The Next Step to Stop it', *Sunday Times*, 15 February 1987.
44. A. C. Srivastava *et al.*, 'Identity Cards for Patients Infected with HIV', 1987, 294 *BMJ*, p. 495.
45. *Chatterton* v. *Gerson* [1980] 3 WLR 1003.
46. *Devi* v. *West Midlands Area Health Authority* [1980] 7CL 44.
47. Medical Defence Union, *AIDS – Medico-Legal Advice*, 1988.
48. M. Sherrard and I. Gatt, 'Human Immunodeficiency Virus (HIV) Antibody Testing', 1987, 295 *BMJ*, p. 911.
49. 'AIDS Monitor', *New Scientist*, 23 July 1987, p. 23.
50. Stephen Cook, 'Go-ahead For Mass AIDS Tests', *Guardian*, 24 November 1988.

51. Raanan Gillon, 'Testing for HIV Without Permission' 1987, 294 *BMJ*, p. 821.
52. Letter by C. A. Carne *et al.*, *Lancet*, 4 July 1987, which concluded that the prevalence rate of HIV-seropositivity based on those consenting to test does not accurately reflect the true rate of seropositivity, but seriously underestimates it.
53. Albert R. Jonsen, Molly Cook and Barbara A. Koenig, 'AIDS and Ethics', 1986, II, Issues in Science and Technology No. 2, p. 56: they note the establishment of a Texan group, Physicians Against AIDS, which demands this.
54. David J. Robinson, Jr, 'AIDS and the Criminal Law: Traditional Approaches and a New Statutory Proposal', 1985, 14 *Hofstra LR* p. 91.
55. Michael Kirby, 'The Five Commandments for New Legislation on AIDS' (a paper given at the 3rd International Conference on AIDS, June 1987).
56. Robinson, 'AIDS and the Criminal Law'.
57. [1888] 22 QBD 23.
58. Gerard Farlin and Piers Wauchope 'AIDS and the Criminal Law', *Law Society's Gazette*, 25 March 1987, p. 884.
59. Gerald H. Gordon, *The Criminal Law of Scotland* (Edinburgh: W. Green and Son, 2nd edn, 1978) paras. 29–48.
60. *Khaliq* v. *HMA* 1984 SLT 137.
61. 'New York Killer's Defense: His Lover Had AIDS', *International Herald Tribune*, 6 March 1987.
62. *D. P. P.* v. *Fountain* [1988] Crim LR 123 and *R.* v. *Fisher* [1987] Crim LR 334.
63. *R.* v. *Malcolm* [1988] Crim LR 189.
64. D. H. J. Hermann, 'Torts: Private Lawsuits About Aids', in Harlon Dalton and S. Burris (eds), *AIDS and the Law: a Guide for the Public* (Yale University Press, 1987) ch. 11.
65. *Kathleen R.-v.-Robert B.* 150 Cal App 3d 992 (1984). More recently and more significantly there has been the Rock Hudson estate litigation – see Ivor Davies, 'Hudson's lover is awarded damages of $8.5 million', *The Times*, 17 February 1989. The traditional position is stated by John G. Fleming, *The Law of Torts* (Sydney: Law Book Co. Ltd. 7th edn, 1987) p. 75, in which he cites the old case of *Hegarty-v.-Shine* (1878) 4 *LR Ir* 288, where a mistress sued her lover for infecting her with venereal disease, but lost her claim partly because there was no legally enforceable duty of disclosure and partly because this was tainted by the 'meretricious nature of her relationship'.
66. Marc A. Franklin, 'Tort Liability for Hepatitis: An Analysis and a Proposal', 1972, 24 *Stanford LR*, p. 439.
67. 551 P 2d 340 (1976).
68. Hancock and Carim, *Deadly Epidemic*, p. 91.
69. Jonsen *et al.*, 'AIDS and Ethics'.
70. The leading case is the House of Lords decision in *Re F* 1989, 139 *N. L. J.*, p. 789.
71. Frances Gibb, 'Wanted: Guardians for the New Jeanettes', *The Times*, 24 June 1987.

72. James Rachels, *The End of Life: Euthanasia and Morality* (Oxford University Press, 1986) pp. 168–9.
73. In England and Wales this is established by the Suicide Act 1961; for Scotland, see Neil Gow, 'Legal Aspects of Suicide', 1958 *SLT* (News) 141.
74. P. Foot, 'Euthanasia', 1977, 6, *Philosophy and Public Affairs*, p. 111.
75. Bayer *et al.*, 'An Ethical Framework'.
76. For example, Arthur S. Leonard, 'AIDS and Employment Law Revisited', 1985, 14, *Hofstra LR*, p. 11.
77. 29 USC §§. 701–96 (1982).
78. Cited by Matthews and Neslund, 'Initial Impact', p. 348.
79. *School Board of Nassau County* v. *Arline* 107 S.Ct. 1123 (1987).
80. Department of Employment/Health and Safety Executive, *AIDS and Employment* (1986)
81. Neil Fagan and David Newell, 'AIDS and Employment Law', 1987, 137 *NLJ*, p. 752.
82. John Hedley, 'Sickness, AIDS and Employment', *Pharmaceutical Journal*, 18 July, 1987, p. 83.
83. This was the investigation by the Equal Opportunities Commission into Dan Air's policy regarding the recruitment of male cabin staff; see C. Southern and G. Howard, *AIDS and Employment Law* (London: Financial Training Publications, 1988) pp. 46–9.
84. John, K. Iglehart, 'Health Policy Report: Financing the Struggle Against AIDS', 1987, 317 *New Eng J Med*, p. 180.
85. B. Shatz, 'The AIDS Insurance Crisis: Underwriting or Overreaching?', 1987, 100 *Harvard LR*, p. 1782.
86. K. A. Clifford and R. P. Luculano, 'AIDS and Insurance: The Rationale for AIDS–Related Testing', 1987, 100 *Harvard LR*, p. 1806.
87. 130 Misc 2d 398, 502 NYS 2d 325 (Supreme Court 1986) and the case is considered at some length by Frederick A. O. Schwarz, Jr and Frederick P. Schaffer, 'AIDS in the Classroom', 1985, 14 *Hofstra LR*, p.163.
88. Dept of Education and Science and Welsh Office, 'Children at School and problems related to AIDS' (March 1986).
89. D. Steele, 'Scots AIDS girl backed on first day at primary', *Glasgow Herald*, 19 August 1988.
90. See John Warden, 'Politicians take over AIDS', 1986, 293 *BMJ*, p.1383.
91. Medical Defence Union, 'Medico-Legal Advice', pp. 17–18.
92. See note 50.
93. See note 32. This policy has not been without its critics; for example, Larry Gostin and William J. Curran, 'AIDS Screening, Confidentiality, and the Duty to Warn', 1987, 77, *American Journal of Public Health*, p.361.
94. Bayer *et al.*, 'An Ethical Framework'.
95. According to the Centers for Disease Control, heterosexual transmission of the virus in the United States is mostly from intravenous drug-users (75 per cent) – A. R. Moss, 'AIDS and Intravenous Drug use: The Real Heterosexual Epidemic', 1987, 294 *BMJ*, p.389.

96. 'Shared Needles Spread AIDS to Heterosexuals', *New Scientist*, 11 June 1987, p. 27.

97. S. E. Barton, D. Taylor-Robinson and J. R. W. Harris, 'Female Prostitutes and Sexually Transmitted Diseases', 1987, 38, *Brit J. Hosp Med*, p.34.

98. David J. Temple, 'AIDS: Facts for Pharmacists', *Pharmaceutical Journal*, 25 April 1987, p. 537.

99. Moss, 'AIDS and Intravenous Drug Use'.

100. See note 87.

101. See note 35.

Part III

The Personal Perspective

10 Coping with the Threat of Death

Anthony Coxon

'Living with your death can clarify the path of your life and increase the quality of satisfaction with living.' (Don Clark, *Living Gay*, 1979)

These words come at the end of a book by an American counsellor to gay people long before the spectre of AIDS came to terrify the gay community, and yet they apply equally well now as then. It is just that the immediacy of the problem is heightened.

Reflecting on what it means to be a gay or bisexual man (I use the term 'gay' inclusively from now on) with the threat of extermination becoming a real possibility, I am struck by the similarity to Weber's characterisation of the Calvinist facing the ultimate question, 'Am I of the elect?'. From a previous situation of comforting and comprehensible simplicity, uncertainty now rules: all the earlier sanctions and grounds of behaviour and expectation disappear. No privileged organisation exists to provide the security of the ark of salvation, no 'assured means of grace' to reassure when belief wavers. The existential message is: 'There is nothing that you can do, and nothing that anyone can do for you which avails aught: you're on your own'.

Perhaps the parallel is too dramatic; perhaps there *is* more that a gay man can do now than the earlier Calvinist could. None the less, the possibility of an early death, and of a death of far greater horror and pain than the most lurid versions of mediaeval Hell could portray, are becoming something which gay men are having to learn to deal with daily. Death (in the United States, if not yet here) is becoming a fact of life for the gay community. Given the long incubation period (so what was then done unwittingly can negate even such an extreme present response as total celibacy), the shortening of the odds of

143

survival as time goes on, the realistic fear that if gross bodily malfunction does not hit, then early dementia will, the increasing experience of seeing one's network of friends decimated in a way that only used to accompany extreme old age – and above all the knowledge that now and in the foreseeable future we are dealing with an incurable disease – all these interact to produce a horrific, even apocalyptic, vision of a gay man's future, should he prove seropositive.

There are two particular points at which the gay man confronts issues of death: (i) When considering the HIV antibody test, and the possibility of seropositivity; and (ii) if full clinical AIDS is diagnosed, in contemplating suicide or euthanasia. I shall look at these, and then go on to look at the consequences of AIDS for gay identity. A main resource I shall use in this will be some recent findings of the pilot study in the Project on Sexual Lifestyles of Non-heterosexual Males, so some preliminary description may be useful.[1] I hasten to add that, with the number involved in the pilot, the data can be no more than suggestive, but that more recent preliminary findings from the main investigation of Project SIGMA (Socio-sexual Investigations of Gay Men and AIDS) support the earlier results.

THE PROJECT

Project SIGMA was initially set up to investigate in reliable detail the current sexual life-styles and related behaviour of homosexual and bisexual (including married) males in London and two other areas with sizeable gay populations at some distance from the capital, Cardiff and Newcastle-upon-Tyne.

All recent sociological studies have emphasised the multiplicity and heterogeneity of styles of homosexual living, which are at least as many and varied as the available styles of heterosexual life. Sexual behaviour (both in terms of the number of sexual contacts and in the range of sexual practices that a man has) is clearly linked to his style of life. Clinical studies assume that risk of transmission of HIV is highest for those with a wide range of partners and with a certain repertoire of sexual practice, but there is no consensus, either within the scientific community or, indeed, amongst gays as to what constitutes a 'wide' range of partners or, by extension, what is an acceptable or 'safe' number. Nor, indeed, is there any reliable information about even such basic facts as what proportion of gay men engage in high-risk activities such as anal intercourse. This project has been designed to provide the basic or baseline data on which such assessments can realistically be founded.

In the present context the problems of sampling and study design and of data collection in such a sensitive and indeed prurient area are crucial, but are not relevant here, although I have considered them elsewhere;[2] here I want rather to draw upon material dealing with psychological and sociological aspects of health, well-being and response to the test.

THE HIV ANTIBODY TEST AND THE THREAT OF SEROPOSITIVITY

While the methodology is not the main issue, it is important to point out that the sample is *not* a clinical one. Indeed, what evidence we currently have underlines the fact that data based on clinical samples do not generalise to the whole of the gay community. The second point is that a major discriminating factor over a very wide range of behaviour and responses turns out to be *how happy a homosexual man is with his orientation* – how far he has come to terms with it, how integrated his sexuality is with the rest of his life. This is nothing new: the important American study by Bell and Weinberg[3] underlined it dramatically, showing how basically it differentiated styles of living and a range of psychological factors. It has not been difficult to detect the same in the United Kingdom, but it is worth stressing that a number of things associated with the transmission of the virus are also differentiated in terms of Acceptance of Gay Identity.

These include the reliance on casual sex and a large number of anonymous sexual partners; the fact of being heterosexually married (but not bisexual identity itself); the number of people who know the sexual identity of the subject and so on. I do not need to spell out the significance of all this for transmission of the virus; I ought perhaps to add that the most risky sexual acts such as anal intercourse, however, are *not* thus differentiated.

In some highly covert areas of homosexual behaviour there is not infrequently a curious and dangerous form of reasoning that 'Because I am not gay and because AIDS is a "gay plague", what I do cannot be risky'. This could be viewed as an unintended consequence of some journalistic treatment of the issue as concerning a social category of gays rather than an orientation-blind virus.

A prevalent ideology among gays is that there is no need to take the HIV antibody test: since the wise man will adopt safer sex practices anyway, taking the test will not affect his behaviour. Like many official accounts, this is more a pious hope than an actuality and a goodly number of gay men take the test precisely to find out whether they *need* to adopt safer sex measures. In the decision, Acceptance of Gay Identity hardly features; the reasons adduced for and against taking the test are complex. By contrast, Acceptance of Gay Identity features strongly in understanding different responses to learning of one's seropositivity. Others are in a better position than I to assess what happens from the point of view of the clinic;[4] organisations such as Body Positive are better equipped to comment on support and help where seroconversion has occurred and is known; the viewpoint here is that of the subjects in the pre-test sample, before, during and after deciding about whether to take the test.

Having decided to take the test, and having been counselled beforehand at the clinic, the person then often goes through an elaborate rehearsal in his own mind of the outcome, and how he will respond to it. The form it takes is strongly influenced by what he knows and believes not only about the test, but about AIDS and about other people's reactions. Apart from anything else, the person envisaging an outcome of seropositivity who is unhappy with his orientation or closeted has also to learn whether and how to develop support relations. Having to come to terms with too far-reaching consequences for one's identity can well impose a strain which is life-threatening. The 'rehearsal' can even take a realistic dramatic form in some cases, where lovers' reactions are tested out by announcing the result as positive. That alone can precipitate a suicide attempt, and is a two-edged sword, since the lover is unlikely to trust again when so vital an outcome has been (in his view) simulated.

Taking the test and finding that one is negative is often claimed to be a reason in itself for taking the test – 'the last chance' to amend one's sexual ways – and so it is for many gay men, but usually only for a time. The lifting of the immediate threat of death (for thus it is often perceived) results in a whole range of other reactions, whose significance and consequences are hard to determine. The reactions include the following:

(a) It can be used as 'proof' to others of one's safeness as a partner (and therefore be a prelude to resuming unsafe sex).
(b) It can be a relief that 'providence' (in some sense) is guarding one, however much one's behaviour ought to have merited a positive result (and therefore again be a support to continuing with risky practices).
(c) It can lead to 'overkill' – rejecting all homosexual behaviour to maintain one's status as seronegative. This is likely to occur among married men and some bisexuals – once again, particularly among those unhappy with their homosexual identity and, once again, a decision that is unlikely to be persevered in, leading to the guilt/infection spiral.

It is not surprising that it is often the *second* test whose outcome is the more feared.

A *positive* result is more momentous; but here again a whole range of reactions are in evidence, from a highly dangerous and irresponsible fatalistic hedonism ('If I've got it, I might just as well go out and enjoy the remaining time') to a cessation of sexual activity, with a similar range of responses to the negative result – and, of course, the modification of one's life-style and coming to terms with one's seropositivity.

The relative frequency of these responses is very hard to gauge; the point here is to stress that a wide range of outcomes other than the preferred or 'rational' ones are both possible and likely. Nor are suicide attempts obviously located, it seems, at predictable points; on this we await more detailed empirical and clinical data. But, grisly and unwelcome as it may be, it seems that one event *does* precipitate major change in sexual life-style; the death from AIDS of a lover or close friend. Unfortunately, before this occurs, the diffusion of the virus is widespread in the at-risk community, and such change produces little overall effect – hence the emphasis on changing sexual patterns now – and the usually forlorn appeal for funding now, while there is time.

SUICIDE AND VOLUNTARY EUTHANASIA

Published systematic data about suicide attempts and voluntary euthanasia in this context is hard to come by, and largely refers to the period before the advent of AIDS. Regrettably, clinical and counselling texts often contain highly tendentious and undemonstrated assertions about homosexual identity *per se* being conducive to suicide attempts. This *may* be true of those unhappy with their identity; I cannot pretend we know. But certainly, even before AIDS it appeared that gay men were more prone to such attempts than heterosexual men. Data worth reproducing show this clearly (see Table 10.1), and our more recent data broadly confirm this.

Table 10.1   Suicidal feelings and impulses

	Suicide	White homo. %	Males White hetero. %	Black homo. %
0	Never imagined	26.0	43.0	37.0
1	Imagined but never seriously considered	37.0	44.0	39.0
2	Seriously considered, but never attempted	19.0	10.0	4.0
3	Attempted at least once	18.0	3.0	20.0

Source: A. P. Bell and M. S. Weinberg, *Homosexualities* (New York: Simon & Schuster, 1978) pp. 450 –1, Table 21.2 and 201–4.

For our purposes, it is relevant, first, to comment that the major contrast is actually between Black and White rather than between homosexual and heterosexual. (The distribution for

black heterosexual males is: 77/21/0/2, but the Black Heterosexual numbers are rather low for stable estimates.) That said,
the main contrast of interest is between (2) and (3), those who
have *seriously considered* and *attempted* suicide (they are
exclusive alternatives here).

Among those who have only *considered* suicide, the reasons
(or the reported reasons) were not usually connected with their
homosexuality, but much more often a result of difficulties
with lovers and an inability to establish meaningful relationships. The situation changes dramatically with the fairly large
percentage who have *attempted* suicide. The attempt occurred
predominantly when they were young (late teens and early
twenties), and the first attempt had overwhelmingly to do with
their inability to accept their homosexuality, as well as with
unstable relationships.

How far this generalises to the United Kingdom, and to the
AIDS generation is moot. But, in any event, the evidence we
have suggests again that those who are unhappy with their
sexual orientation are above all the most likely to attempt
suicide.

In my own opinion – and I must stress here that it is nothing
more – a far more important issue than suicide as response to
seropositivity or a diagnosis of AIDS or ARC is the question of
how voluntary euthanasia should be discussed in this context.
For obvious reasons, the incidence of requests for life-
termination is rarely mentioned in the clinical literature, yet it
is something which should be rationally discussed. A person
knowing his diagnosis, and reasonably informed about the
prognosis and likely developments, might make the informed
decision either to commit suicide or to have the means to do so
if he considers his situation intolerable. (I know of a number of
gay men who keep lethal drugs in their bathroom cabinets,
much as some others do in case of nuclear war.)

The same considerations apply here, I think, as with
voluntary euthanasia in general, but with one important
difference. The dividing line between 'encouraged' or
'colluded-in' suicide and homocide is a thin one, as anyone
who has seen *BENT* or *The Normal Heart* will know. There are
enough people of ill-will (unfortunately present in the nursing,
medical and clerical professions) who view seropositivity or
any AIDS-related conditions as 'self-inflicted' or as retribution

for a deviant identity or life-style to make the decision perilously close to one taken under pressure.

COPING WITH DEATH, REVISITED

The title of this chapter implicitly makes reference to the gay man; it can equally well be interpreted to refer to the wider community, medical and political. How do *they* cope with the situation? The immediate answer has to be 'Not well.' It is very hard not to cry 'Too little, too late' or do a Cassandra when one sees the opportunities to take action repeatedly, regularly and continually thrown away; 'I told you so' is not considered a measured response, but it is a realistic one. There is neither the political will nor even the political sympathy to respond realistically – or even in terms of society's long-term financial interest, which is more striking.

It also needs to be said that the necessary research is often highly unbalanced. Now of course medical research and treatment is a crucial and central part of the battle to contain and cure AIDS and related conditions, and of course there are many physicians who devote their time and talents far beyond the call of duty. But too often, in the United Kingdom especially, a form of medical hegemony comes to dominate the whole area. Defining the condition, and prescribing the means of alleviation and control, are undeniably and manifestly medical matters, but setting limits to 'acceptable (sexual) behaviour', commending changes in manner of life and helping people to come to terms with their condition (and orientation) are not. Today I perceive far greater clericalism in the medical profession than in the ministry.

But of course, AIDS and seropositivity are far more than a medical issue; they profoundly affect people and their relationships and lives, and their consequences are as appalling in the social and economic spheres as they are in the medical. In the sociological and psychological areas the competences required are not medical and are sometimes hindered by medical attitudes and orientations. The complexities and subtleties needed are of a different kind and order; it is no safer here than in medical matters to rely on British gentlemanly amateurism. Yet, comparing the medical and social sciences, the imbalance in funding and support is stark and puzzling. Above all else it hinders our understanding of what is happening, and the monitoring of the way people are responding to health education and personal crises. I find it highly ironical that, in an area where enormous efforts are made to ensure that drugs are monitored and evaluated, it is assumed that health education needs no such evaluation and monitoring. I think it fair to say that only under considerable pressure have self-help groups such as the Terrence Higgins Trust and Body Positive received any funding, and then the level has been pathetic in comparison to need (and performance). We have become accustomed, I suppose, to governmental action which is purely responsive to crises and which enthrones financial self-help as a prime virtue, but the irony is that even on these terms the present policies are counter-productive. Lack of funding now means not simply more deaths, but also unnecessary deaths and grossly more expensive health care costs in the future.

The problems and paradoxes confronting those who themselves confront the reality of imminent death of themselves and their loved ones will increase for some time, no matter what resources are made available, and no matter if the 'community' is involved more centrally in caring, or not. Given the depth of need for people of skill and goodwill, it may seem secondary to insist again on the need to monitor in a disciplined manner the way in which communities that face virtual destruction have coped in the past, and what resources they can bring to the present. It is after all only a matter of a few centuries since the threat of likely and imminent death confronted most people in their maturity, and for a while the same may be true again. Then, as now, preserving the quality of life and the control over one's life and death becomes as important as the search for a vaccine.

Notes

1.   A.P.M. Coxon, Report of Pilot Study (Cardiff: University of Wales, College of Cardiff) *Project SIGMA Working Paper no. 2*, 1986.

2. See Tony Coxon, ' "Something Sensational . . ": the sexual diary as a tool for mapping detailed sexual behaviour', *Sociological Review*, 36, 2, 1988, pp. 353–67.
3. A. P. Bell and M. S. Weinberg, *Homosexualities* (New York: Simon & Schuster, 1978).
4. David Miller, 'Psychology, AIDS, ARC AND PGL', in D. Miller, J. Weber and J. Green (eds), *The Management of AIDS Patients* (London: Macmillan, 1985).

11 AIDS: Some Theological Reflections

Anthony Lovegrove

> If today the plague is in your midst, that is because the hour has struck for taking thought. The just man need have no fear, but the evil-doer has good cause to tremble. For the plague is the flail of God and the world is His threshing-floor, and implacably He will thresh out His harvest until the wheat is separated from the chaff'.

Thus spake Father Paneloux during this first sermon in Camus' *The Plague*.[1] Whenever an earthquake devastates a city, a bridge collapses or a disease rages, there will inevitably be someone around who voices sentiments similar to those contained in Paneloux's sermon. AIDS is no exception. There have been some Christians who have seen God's punishment of our world in the spread of AIDS, and some who almost appear to be pleased that God has at last picked up His flail. That the same people do not see the hand of God at work on those who, for example, die of lung cancer as a result of smoking, or sclerosis of the liver as a result of over-indulgence in drink, does not strike them as at all illogical or odd. Neither do such Christians find it incongruous that their founder was notorious for welcoming all those whom his society called outcasts, quite regardless of whether or not that society branded them as sinners.

At the outset of these few reflections it is very important to establish that it is in no way theologically legitimate to echo the words of Paneloux. Since AIDS was first identified in the United States in 1981 it has not infrequently been called a plague, or the 'gay plague', and AIDS sufferers have been branded as lepers. Naturally AIDS has given rise to great anxiety and considerable fear everywhere, largely because there was, and still is in some quarters, a lot of ignorance about it. There is always fear of the unknown, and the more so when the illness has such terrible effects and is at the moment incurable.

Inaccurate and intemperate language only serves to accent-uate the fear and anxiety which society has about AIDS, and happily with the passage of time and the dissemination of more accurate information there is beginning to be found a more balanced approach. Reading articles dated in the autumn of 1986 one can detect a change in the climate. Reporting in *The Tablet* on 8 November 1986, on a conference held at Spode Conference Centre at the beginning of that month, Timothy Radcliffe said: 'the Church will only be able to respond in the proper way [to AIDS] if we resist the tide of fear and hysteria which is accompanying the spread of AIDS . . . but . . . it has always been the job of the Church to take a stand against superstition and mythology'. Sadly the Church has not always lived up to that task, but there are signs today that considerable efforts are being made to approach this disease in a truly Christian way. The conference ended with the unanimous approval of a statement: 'Our Lord came to redeem mankind, healing the sick and identifying with the outcast. We, the Church, his disciples who seek to carry on his work and to be like him, can only show ourselves his followers if we too share in the love of God for those in need'.

It would seem, therefore, that at the outset there should be a move to offer all AIDS sufferers immense compassion and help. Such an attitude would extend as well to the family and friends of those who are suffering, because they are most clearly the next in line for help. There has to be a definite move to ensure that those who suffer from AIDS themselves do not feel isolated and rejected, because first reactions from those around are frequently going to lead to such a situation. If we are to be able to offer both compassion and help, the first requirement is that we be clear about the illness and seek to know the truth about it as well as about the way it is spread. Avoiding the use of dramatic language, it is helpful to be reminded that AIDS is 'simply another infectious illness ("infectious" in that it is passed from one person to another or others in certain limited situations)'.[2] Then, with the help of medical knowledge, the temptation to brand AIDS as the 'homosexual plague' will be avoided. Because of ignorance there has been a tendency for some to see AIDS solely in terms of homosexuality, and so the reaction in some quarters has been a moral backlash spurred on by a deep disgust. The truth is that AIDS is an illness which affects both homosexuals and heterosexuals. Once this is grasped some of the self-righteous recrimination evaporates. The danger is that prejudice will affect our thinking and behaviour if we focus attention on the way in which the illness spread most rapidly at the beginning of this decade in the United States, and more recently in the United Kingdom. The average group of Christians, made up of a cross-section of different denominations, will be split in its attitude towards homosexuality. Theological reflections about AIDS will certainly mirror that division, and the Churches' Occasional Paper, referred to earlier, noted that the working party, having recorded the divergence on homosexuality, set it aside 'because AIDS and homosexuality are two different matters'.[3] Initially any theological reflections will be concerned with the sufferers, and those sufferers are our fellow human beings, men, women and children. When confronted with anyone who is suffering from any disease the natural attitude ought to be one of compassion. When that illness is as devastating in its consequences as AIDS then that compassion should be all the greater. Genuine compassion leads to help, and it is here that our knowledge is equally significant.

Prudence is sometimes thought to be the queen of virtues, and so terms like 'plague' can be the cause of would-be helpers pleading prudence and refusing to help. The medical evidence supports the view that ordinary contact does not lead to infection, yet some Christians have been loath to accept this and so refuse to drink from the chalice at the Holy Communion. What many people will remember about the life of Francis of Assisi, who had the normal fear of any mediaeval person of leprosy, is that when he met a leper one day he went up and hugged and kissed him to assure him that he was not an outcast. Later on, when he went to work at the local lazar-house among the lepers, his care and help served to bring home to those people that they were not rejected by their society, even if, as a result of the nature of the disease, they were isolated from society. What Francis, and others like him, did was considerably more hazardous than the act of the communicant who receives the chalice after an AIDS sufferer has just drunk from the same cup. Compassion and caring will become very difficult if our initial attitude is to distance ourselves from the patient, and this is all the more sad when we subsequently discover that there was no danger of being infected.

Compassion and help turn more swiftly to care once the risk of infection has been correctly diagnosed, and already much consideration has been given to problems of pastoral care. At the outset plans to set up residential care centres for AIDS sufferers, both in the United States and in the United Kingdom, met with strong opposition. Even when the necessary funds have been obtained it has proved difficult to acquire a building because petitions with hundreds of signatories delay the permission needed to begin work. 'Wouldn't it be better if these people were out in the country? At least they could look at a bit of greenery in their final days' is not an untypical response. As mentioned earlier, it has 'always been the job of the Church to take a stand against superstition and mythology' and the popular reaction, fomented in some instances by irresponsible journalism and intemperate language, needs to be swiftly countered and positively rejected. As more and more medical evidence is published it becomes apparent that earlier fears about the risk of infection were unjustified, and it is to be hoped that in a calmer atmosphere compassion will be given a chance. Truth will always remain near to the forefront of any theological reflections, and the interpretation, as well as the presentation, of facts plays a vital role in the human response.

The approach of most governments has been to stress prevention, in the absence, as yet, of any cure. While research into a cure is being funded world-wide, and in some places even co-ordinated so as to avoid duplication, clearly the main campaign has to be waged via prevention. In the United Kingdom, for example, the government's policy has been to focus attention on people knowing the facts so that they do not die as a result of ignorance. As so often happens with campaigns directed towards the spread of information it is almost impossible to discover how well and how widely the message has been received. The presentation of the message has also to be altered to prevent a familiarity which can trigger a person's just switching off, in every sense of the term. To date not only has every home received a leaflet through the post, but there have been television presentations, though at least one 'advert' was criticised for being too arcane. Perhaps the whole approach needs to be more carefully considered and the accent moved away from fear. Is fear the right emotion to be aroused when knowledge and truth are being demanded? It can be argued that the creation of fear is precisely the wrong way to tackle the issue as it tends to block clear thinking. Bear in mind that it is because of fear that people with AIDS are likely to experience the further suffering of rejection and isolation, instead of the compassion and help which they need.

Since AIDS has become the main concern of the medical world it is natural that more and more funding should be given to research into a cure, though from all accounts the immediate prognosis is not very encouraging. In the hope of a breakthrough being made there are a number of further considerations to be made. Has the emergence of AIDS raised any questions about our understanding of ourselves as human beings? Will the discovery of a cure mean that everything is as it was before AIDS made its appearance?

So far these reflections have centred on our response to people with AIDS, and the focus has been on compassion and help, and on the needs of those suffering from AIDS. All along there has been a plea for the spread of genuine and reliable information. So that the truth about AIDS may be grasped more accurately by everyone it is important that the flow of information be continually updated, that the public should not be confronted with conflicting information, and that the accent be taken off any presentation which is likely to foster fear. As information about the way that AIDS is spread is also of the utmost importance, the truth about that must also be given. As in all matters of life and death, the truth about the facts becomes all the more urgent. To mislead people with half-truths, to hold back information on whatever pretext, to cloud the message in any way, is both wrong and immoral. But reflections can also be offered on the way in which the disease is transmitted, especially since, at the moment, in the absence of any cure, the prevention of the spread of the disease depends on the way each one of us behaves. Men and women are being asked to behave towards each other in ways that are responsible, and that is right. But who decides what degree of responsibility is called for and indeed what constitutes responsibility in the first place?

To date the campaign against AIDS has been waged in terms of the need to take precautions, with emphasis placed on the use of condoms, which has become identified with 'safe sex'. However, recent research on condoms has revealed that they are by no means 100 per cent safe, and now there is a call for an even more rigorous process of inspection at the very moment when there is a huge increase in the demand for them. Furthermore evidence seems to indicate that some lack of success with condoms is due to inexperience, and this particularly among the young who are just the age group which is very much at risk. How honest is it to imply that 'safe sex' is to be identified with the use of condoms? It would seem that there has been a short-circuiting of the question about responsibility in the area of human sexuality. To promote the use of condoms as first-line defence against the spread of AIDS would seem to fall below the level of response which is called for.

These few reflections are too brief to allow for a lengthy treatise or investigation into our society's understanding of the function and purpose of sex, but no treatment would be complete without some mention. It is undeniable that any couple who come together when uninfected by AIDS, and whose relationship is marked by fidelity, will not acquire the disease as a result of their sexual activity. It is true that either one or both of them might acquire the virus through an infected batch of blood if a blood transfusion has been necessary, or via an infected needle, or indeed from transplantation of skin or organs, but it is generally agreed that, with the exception of drug abusers employing the same needle, these are not the main ways in which the disease is spread. Whether the couple who come together are hetero- or homosexual, if they are uninfected at the beginning of their relationship, then they will not acquire the virus as a result of their sexual activity. What is apparent from recent studies is that promiscuity has led to a rapid spread of the disease, and because of the lengthy period of incubation people who have already contracted AIDS are unaware that they have it, and so do not realise that they are passing it on to others. A radical change in outlook towards sexual behaviour is necessary if the progress of AIDS is to be halted, and given the present climate this will not be easy. Few, however, would deny that we are moral agents, and that society expects us to take responsibility for our conduct. For Socrates the 'unreflecting life is not worth living', and to live in a society means that we must consider the implications of what we do. I should not drive my car with no regard for other road users, or only drive with care when I see that there are police around. Given what we now know about the dangers of smoking, I should be considerate towards others if I choose to smoke. To disregard the health of others would be wrong. Does this attitude not also extend to sex? It is a tragedy that something like AIDS has to come along before we make any attempt to be morally sensitive about our sexual behaviour.

Borrowing Camus' device in *The Plague* we might ask Father Paneloux to preach another sermon after he has been working in a hospice for people with AIDS. We might envisage him saying:

If today AIDS is in your midst then the hour has struck for a genuine Christian response. AIDS is not the flail of God, nor is the world His threshing-floor. We must not be judgemental of those who suffer from AIDS, but must try to help them. They are men and women like you and like me, who need our love and care and the help of our society. We will not catch AIDS from those we help or nurse if we follow sensible rules. What we will catch is an awareness of their loneliness and their rejection by many of our fellow men and women. What those who suffer from AIDS will also teach us is that we need to think about our own attitude to sex. Our society can all too easily focus attention solely on sexual pleasure and fail to place sex within a loving relationship. As Christians we believe that sexual relations only have true meaning in the context of human love – a love which is ideally a lifelong union in which two people give themselves totally and exclusively one to the other. We may not find it easy to accept this, and it is not always easy to live such a loving relationship, but it will enrich us as human beings, and will also offer real protection against AIDS.

Notes

1.   A. Camus, *The Plague* (Harmondsworth: Penguin, 1960) p. 80.
2.   'A Christian Comment on AIDS', *The Churches' Council for Health and Healing, Occasional Papers*, 1986, no. 6.
3.   Ibid., p. 2.

12 Personal Issues and Personal Dilemmas

Brenda Almond

Some of the problems raised by AIDS are unique to this disease – the combination of its deadly nature and the fact that it is most prominently a sexually transmitted complaint give rise to a range of problems not encountered before in combination. It is often said that the taboos of earlier generations about sex have been replaced in the current generation with a taboo about death. An issue which combines elements of these potent subjects inevitably presents itself to people in the late nineteen-eighties as a unique and difficult challenge.

As the various contributions to this book have shown, this challenge has many aspects – legal, political, social – which need to be shaped, structured and informed by an ethical perspective. But it is at the personal rather than the community level that the individual must confront a range of new and inevitably painful ethical choices. These will differ for the person with AIDS, the person testing positive for HIV infection, and persons free of infection at various ages and stages of life.

To take this last group first, those living in settled monogamy may seem to have little to fear. For them, AIDS may seem to be a problem for other people. But if they assume this they will be ignoring the overwhelming evidence of history and literature that, where sexual relationships are concerned, no one can be wholly sure of another person's fidelity. And, since the coming of AIDS, for both partners secret unfaithfulness carries a lethal potentiality. Many people have alleviated the strains of a long relationship – indeed may in their own minds have enhanced and preserved that relationship – by conducting a relationship or relationships outside its boundaries. And not only relationships: traditionally, prostitution has provided an outlet for pent-up frustrations, or for sexual tendencies not catered for in normal heterosexual marriage. To take one example only, the risk posed by a bisexual to his wife was, before AIDS, emotional only: supposing that he cared for her happiness, discovery would have seemed the greatest threat to that happiness. But in a situation in which every external liaison might bring exposure to an infection which could be active but latent for months or years, the risk placed on the unknowing partner is a risk in another dimension altogether: it is nothing less than the risk of death.

It is clear, then, that the ethical imperative for those involved in activities outside a central relationship must be the 'safer sex' norm, though even here one is accepting for another person a risk they personally would probably *not* accept or take. Hence what may have seemed morally justified in the past can only under these circumstances be *less morally objectionable* than either honesty and openness (*informing* the partner of the central relationship, thus giving that partner autonomy as far as the risk-taking choice is concerned) or avoiding all external encounters altogether.

But the moral dilemmas of the sexually-established or the middle-aged are likely to be less intrusive than the dilemmas posed by AIDS for their children. And it is through their children that their own lives are most likely to be touched by this illness. For the sexual revolution is so much a feature of contemporary life in liberal societies that there are now few young people who expect their first sexual relationship to be their only one. This may still feature as an ideal for either the romantic or the religious but, even as an ideal, it is clear that it leaves an often unacceptable role to be played by luck and circumstance.

Happier marriages may well be based on the wider knowledge and understanding that results from a richer variety of relationships and of sexual experience. But if the young are to experiment, how are they to do this safely in the AIDS era? Some 'unsafe' experimentation is bound to precede the competent and self-confident handling of 'safer sex' methods as a key to unlocking this conundrum. But certainly sex education will have to include the sort of detailed and specific technical instruction in barrier protection that would have seemed neither desirable nor necessary for contraceptive purposes alone (the contraceptive pill obviating the need for cruder old-fashioned methods). As far as these methods are concerned, the churches' objection here to methods of preventing life should lapse when the same methods are employed for preventing death. So the concept of the condom as a normal accompaniment of sexual intercourse must be promoted positively. People are now beginning to attack the so-called 'condom culture'. They point to the unreliability of condoms and the folly of regarding them as a definitive solution to the AIDS problem. All this is fair comment, but on a public scale condoms must be promoted despite their imperfections. For, while they cannot provide a guarantee for one individual, their widespread use will *statistically* reduce the number of infections. In any case, some protection is clearly better than no protection at all.

The caveat must be that, in promoting condom use, it is necessary to avoid promoting random sexual activity. For experimentation for its own sake, and variety for egotistical reasons, can no longer, if they ever could, find any moral defence. The ethical imperative for the young will be to place an added emphasis on the term 'relationship', and the attempt to reach a stable plateau will be given impetus and momentum by the increased dangers added to this search by the advent of AIDS.

Specifically there will need to be increased awareness of the unacceptable risks involved in random or anonymous sex: the one-night stand; the party encounter; the quick involvement with a stranger. A minimalist message of this sort could usefully be the goal of health educators and teachers involved with sex education who, whatever their own views, are bound to recognise that the advice that the old have so often given to the young – to practise chastity before marriage and mono-gamy within it – will equally often be rejected.

These are problems, then, for the uninfected. What of those who have reason to think they *might* have been infected? The ethical imperatives here can only be arrived at by means of two well-established virtues: honesty and compassion. Honesty dictates that one needs to know, and this is a judgment which cannot be affected by consideration of social or economic consequences beyond the individual's control; compassion or consideration for others dictates that this knowledge is needed so that others are not deliberately put at risk. The only alternative to this is to decide to behave *as if* one had been tested and found positive, consequences that may be unnecessary and unacceptable for a person who is not in fact infected.

What, then, are the ethical consequences of seropositivity? First, it is clearly not necessary to settle for the unrealistic goal of ceasing all sexual activity. By joining organisations set up to help the HIV-positive person, one will encounter other people whose sexual problems are similar, and by sharing of experience and information discover ways to find sexual satisfaction in which no other people will be put at risk. For there *is* an unpalatable ethical imperative here: not to put another at risk without their knowledge. In the case of a deep and strong relationship, a person, once informed, may be willing to take that risk, no doubt under 'safer sex' conditions, but, in the characteristic 'chain' effect caused by AIDS, such persons will themselves be faced with the same dilemmas *vis-à-vis other* people. *They* will have to be prepared to monitor their own HIV status and to inform any other sexual partners. (Of course, if this *is* a deep and strong relationship, no others may be contemplated and the risk therefore confined to one.)

Apart from these problems of personal relations which confront the asymptomatic HIV-positive person, the central preoccupation must, of course, be the possibility, indeed likelihood, of illness. So, finally, what are the ethical problems confronted by someone who knows that he or she has AIDS?

From the point of view of avoiding communicating infection, but at the same time maintaining or developing what will be increasingly important personal relationships, people with AIDS are, of course, in the same position as the HIV-positive person, although it is less likely that concealment of their condition will continue to be a possibility.

For them, however, their medical prognosis is likely to be a central preoccupation. Coming to terms with that prognosis is no easy task. Most will want to co-operate with their medical advisers in overcoming the repeated opportunistic infections that are a feature of this illness, and to maximise their opportunities for work, pleasure and achievement in the meantime. They may be helped in maintaining health, and in coping with illness when it comes, by turning to medicine outside what is conventionally accepted in Western societies. For where technological intervention cannot cure, mental and emotional adaptation may alleviate stress and even physical symptoms. In these circumstances conventional medical practitioners may well be more willing than in other situations to regard holistic or organic approaches as truly *complementary* medicine, and not as an unacceptable alternative. What is more, these approaches may carry with them a complete philosophical stance, familiar in the East, but not unrepresented in Western philosophical traditions from the time of the Stoics, in which understanding and acceptance of the cycle of life brings with it a shift in intellectual and emotional attitude that benefits the body as well as the mind.

The fact must be faced, however, that sooner or later increasingly unpleasant and personality-destroying bodily malfunctions will create a situation of untreatable, if not unalleviable, pain and illness. In this situation the issues of euthanasia and assisted suicide may gain a particular personal urgency. For carers there will be questions about the wise, reasonable or humane limits to treatment, as well as, for the person himself or herself, questions about the right of a dying person, perhaps before the onset of a terminal illness to make, autonomously, a decision about the nature and conditions of his or her own death.

Euthanasia features differently as an issue in relation to AIDS than in its more usual context. In that more familiar context, arguments in favour of euthanasia are usually advanced in relation to the very old, with some limited extension to those who fall tragically victim to accident or illness earlier on. But it is distinctive of AIDS that the questions of euthanasia and assisted suicide must be thought of predominantly in relation to the relatively young – people in their twenties and thirties and in full possession of their faculties. They may well be people with strong views on the subject of suicide and euthanasia in relation to their own condition, and people who feel most strongly their right to take a way out from avoidable suffering. They may also feel better able to cope with their condition if they know that the means of escape are in their own hands.

So where the issue is not the acceptance or rejection of

treatment, but of choosing, in some more direct manner, suicide, there is a strong case for saying that since suicide itself is no longer a criminal matter – that is, it is not itself illegal – individuals have a *right* to commit suicide if their rational assessment of their situation is that that is the best course both for themselves and those close to them. But if there is a right to commit suicide, then, arguably, there is a right to competent medical advice as to how to do this, and to information on obtaining the means, and even perhaps to direct assistance, if this is not contrary to the medical practitioner's own ethical stance. The advent of AIDS makes legal and governmental decisions on this important issue more pressing if decisions are to be placed, where they rightly belong, in the hands of the person confronting the inevitability of death, and wishing to have some control over the manner of it.

Here, then, is the hard base-line in the AIDS issue: the point where, alone, the individual confronts his or her own death. If this is the finishing point for ethics, it is also its starting-point. For the earliest recorded moral philosophy in Western philosophical traditions began with Plato's response to Socrates' approach to his own death. It is important in the case of an issue which raises so many subsidiary ethical questions to remember that the individual's lonely confrontation with death is, and always has been, a central ethical concern.

CONCLUDING COMMENTS

AIDS is a personal issue and an issue for the individual. But, as most of the contributions to this volume have shown, it is also a public and social issue, and new social issues are usually tackled by legislative measures. However law is a blunt instrument for bringing about the enormous changes in behaviour necessary to reduce the threat posed by this new disease. Sex, as the philosopher Santayana said, is nature's categorical imperative, and so people will continue to take enormous risks both with their own health and with that of others under the overwhelming pressure of this drive. It is worth repeating, then, that changes in behaviour that regulate people's sex-lives – fewer partners or, indeed, premarital chastity and faithful monogamy – while they may be recommended, will continue to be honoured as much in the breach as in the observance. Education is, therefore, essential, and indeed it is the only tool available in the absence of cure or vaccine. But it cannot be assumed that everyone will agree about the nature of that education.

Shocked by the implied acceptance of immorality, the religious right in some countries is opposed to sex education in schools, explicit public education campaigns, and most particularly to education and advertising about condoms. They see in AIDS a tool to turn back the wheel of the sexual revolution, and certainly AIDS is a deadly chain-letter for sexually liberated societies. But to those who think like this, it must be said that, historically, good advice has never been lacking, but that it is often the fate of good advice to be ignored, particularly by the young and headstrong. And the young are willing to take risks, even with their lives. Otherwise wars would not have been fought, as they frequently have been, by teenagers and people in their early twenties, nor would the roads of developed nations yield up an annual sacrifice of thousands of young road-users who have not yet learned the caution of their elders, or the unique importance of simply being alive.

So any educational strategy that is to be successful must embrace, as lovingly as do the young themselves, the reality of sexuality. This means not only the forms of sexuality that furnish ideals for literature, poetry and religion, but also sexuality for money, sexuality for release, sexuality for one, sexuality for same-sex partners. Some will find this repugnant, but they will have to ask themselves whether they can take responsibility for the safety of their own young in a world overlaid by the invisible menace of the AIDS virus.

The key and salient need here is to understand the nature of the threat that is posed. This is a virus which attacks us – human beings, that is – in our reproductive function. If there is to be a future for the human race, there must be young people who have never encountered the virus. There must also be people who can know and trust each other enough to keep the threat away from their own relationship, at least for the child-bearing years. For, in this context, 'safe sex' is not an option.

Outside the crucial area of life where sex is intended for generation, the condom, at present, is in a literal sense the only physical barrier and protection from this disease. Moral protection is indeed to be sought as well. But this will come, not from setting unrealistic goals for other people, but from renewed attention to older and more central moral values – values such as honesty, openness and care for each other. In practice, being directed by these values dictates, first, that the facts uncovered by AIDS research, no matter how unpalatable, be confronted by both governments and individuals without prevarication or dissimulation; and, secondly, that policies based on those facts must not ignore the need to protect those so far unaffected from the threat to their life and health posed by this microscopic enemy.

Finally, it means taking account, too, of the claims of future unborn human beings, whose very existence may be in question if nature or science do not quickly restore the old order of things. AIDS, then, *is* a moral issue – one requiring human beings urgently to reach a consensus on the promotion of an appropriate range of moral values: the sort of values which can, like the virus itself, transcend boundaries of culture, class, colour and religion.

An AIDS Bibliography
John Lord

This list is confined to printed publications in the English language: audio-visual materials, such as video programmes, slides and charts have not been included nor have I attempted to record all the many leaflets and booklets that are distributed free of charge.

The literature on AIDS and its implications is now vast, and is scattered through publications on almost every conceivable subject. Moreover the pace at which it is growing outstrips the capacity to keep up to date. I have of necessity had to rely on many standard bibliographical sources in compiling this list, otherwise it would have been very much shorter than it is, and I make no pretence of having inspected all the items that are given here. This is, then, a rather imperfect piece of work. But it is a beginning.

It is not easy to draw definite boundaries in this area, so, as well as the purely ethical and legal questions, I have also included some material which has a bearing on more general social matters.

It is worth noting that, of the various specialised journals on AIDS that are being published, there are two that deal with matters of ethical and legal importance: *AIDS and Public Policy* and *AIDS Policy and Law*. Both commenced publication in 1986.

BIBLIOGRAPHIES (Concerning all Aspects of AIDS)

Abrams, Estelle J., *AIDS Bibliography, 1986–1987* (US Department of Health and Human Services, 1987).

Garoogian, Rhoda, *AIDS, 1981–1983: an Annotated Bibliography*, (Vantage, 1984).

Gosney, Neil and Dianne Mitchell, *AIDS: an Index compiled from the Resources of the City of London Polytechnic Libraries* (City Poly Library Services, 1988).

Health Education Council, *AIDS: Acquired Immune Deficiency Syndrome: Resource List* (Health Education Council, 1986).

McLeod, D. W. and Alan V. Miller, *Medical, Social, and Political Aspects of the AIDS Crisis: a Bibliography* (Canadian Gay Archives, 1985).

Tyckoson, David A., *AIDS: Acquired Immune Deficiency Syndrome*, 2nd edn (Oryx, 1985).

Tyckoson, David A., *AIDS 1987* (Oryx, 1987)

BOOKS AND PAMPHLETS

Items listed here are published in London unless otherwise stated, and are arranged alphabetically under the name of the author, editor or title, as appropriate.

AIDS: The workplace issues (NY: American Management Association, 1985).

Altman, Dennis, *AIDS: Sexuality, Death, and Moral Puritanism* (Pluto, 1986).

Bayer, Ronald, *Private Acts, Social Consequences: AIDS and the Politics of Public Health* (N.Y.: The Free Press, 1989).

Bayles, Michael D., *Reproductive Ethics* (Englewood Cliffs, NJ: Prentice-Hall, 1984).

Becker, M. H. (ed.), *AIDS Education: The Public Health Challenge* (Chichester: Wiley, for the Health Education Quarterly, 1987).

Black, D., *The Plague Years* (Picador, 1986).

Blackie, Duncan and Ian Taylor, *AIDS: The Socialist View* (Bookmarks, 1987).

Brown, R. K., *AIDS, Cancer and the Medical Establishment* (NY: Speller, 1986).

Cahill, K. M. (ed.), *The AIDS Epidemic* (Hutchinson, 1984).

Cantwell, Alan, *AIDS: The Mystery and the Solution*, 2nd edn (Los Angeles: Aries Rising, 1986).

Church of England Board for Social Responsibility, *AIDS: Some Guidelines for Pastoral Care* (Church House, 1986).

Churches' Council for Health and Healing, *A Christian Comment on AIDS* (The Council, 1986).

Collier, Caroline, *The Twentieth-Century Plague* (Oxford: Lion, 1987).

Cosstick, V. (ed.), *AIDS: Meeting the Community Challenge* (Slough: St Paul's Publications, 1987).

Dalton, Harlon and others (eds), *AIDS and the Law: a Guide for the Public* (Yale University Press, 1987).

Denning, John V., *AIDS: The Real Truth about the Acquired Immune Deficiency Syndrome* (Dorking: the author, 1987).

Dornette, W. H. L., *AIDS and the Law*, (Chichester: Wiley, 1987).

Feldman, Douglas A. and Thomas M. Johnson (eds), *Social Dimensions of AIDS* (New York: Praeger, 1986).

Fitzpatrick, Michael and Don Milligan, *The Truth about the AIDS Panic* (Junius, 1987).

Green, John and David Miller, *AIDS: The Story of a Disease* (Grafton, 1986).

Hancock, Graham and Enver Carim, *AIDS: The Deadly Epidemic* (Victor Gollancz, 1986).

Hummel, Robert F. (ed.), *AIDS: Impact on Public Policy; Proceedings of a Conference, New York, 1986* (Plenum, 1986).

Ide, Arthur F., *AIDS Hysteria* (Las Colinas, TX: Monument, 1986).

Institute of Medicine and National Academy of Sciences, *Mobilizing against AIDS: The Unfinished Story of a Virus* (Harvard University Press, 1986).

Kilpatrick, Alison and David Kilpatrick, *AIDS* (Edinburgh: Chambers, 1987).

McKie, Robin, *Panic: The Story of AIDS* (Wellingborough: Thorsons, 1986).

Madhok, R., C. D. Forbes and B. L. Evatt (eds), *Blood Products and AIDS* (Chapman & Hall, 1987).

Masters, W. H., Johnson, V. E. and Kolodny, R. C., *Heterosexual Behaviour in the Age of AIDS* (Weidenfeld and Nicolson, 1988).

Paine, Leslie, *AIDS: Psychiatric and Psychosocial Perspectives* (Croom Helm, 1987).

Panos Institute, *AIDS in the Third World* (Panos Institute, 1986).

Patton, Cindy, *Sex and Germs: the Politics of AIDS* (Boston, MA: South End, 1987).

Pierce, Christine and Donald Van De Veer, *AIDS, Ethics and Public Policy* (Belmont, Calif.: Wadsworth, 1988).

Richardson, Diane, *Women and the AIDS Crisis* (Pandora, 1987).

Robertson, Roy, *Heroin, AIDS and Society* (Sevenoaks: Hodder & Stoughton, 1987).

Shilts, Randy, *And the Band Played On* (Harmondsworth: Penguin, 1988).

Twentieth-Century Task Force on the Communication of Scientific Risk, *Science in the Streets* (NY: Priority, 1984); contains 'AIDS in the media', by Harry Schwartz.

Vass, Antony, A., *AIDS – A Plague in Us: a Social Perspective: the Condition and its Social Consequences* (St Ives: Venus Academica, 1986).

Watney, Simon, *Policing Desire:Pornography, AIDS & the Media* (Methuen, 1987).

Witt, Michael (ed.), *AIDS and Patient Management: Legal, Ethical, and Social Issues* (Owings Mills MD: National Health Publishing, 1986).

ARTICLES FROM PERIODICALS

The articles listed here are to be found in journals and magazines, and also a few newspapers, mainly from the British national press.

'The acquired immune deficiency syndrome: B-cell lymphoma, histoplasmosis, and ethics and economics', *Annals of Internal Medicine*, V104 (1986) pp. 447–8.

Adelmann, H. C., 'AIDS, Sex and Dope: a re-evaluation of ethics and morals', *Ohio Medicine*, V84 (1988) pp. 7, 11.

Adler, Michael W., 'ABC of AIDS: development of the epidemic', *British Medical Journal*, N1083 (1987) pp. 294.

'AIDS: the emerging ethical dilemmas', *Hastings Center Report*, V15(4) Suppl. (1985) pp. 1–32.

Almond, Brenda, 'AIDS: liberty or life?', *The Times*, 16 June 1987, p. 16.

Almond, Brenda, 'Tackling AIDS', *Times Higher Education Supplement*, 4 Mar. 1988, p. 11.

Almond, Brenda, 'AIDS and international ethics', *Ethics and International Affairs*, V2 (1988) pp. 139–54.

Anderson, Digby, 'No moral panic – that's the problem', *The Times*, 18 June 1985, p. 12.

Anderson, Digby, 'Facts that stay concealed', *The Times*, 19 Aug. 1987, p. 10.

Bayer, Ronald, Carol Levine and Susan M. Wolf, 'HIV antibody screening: an ethical framework for evaluating proposed programs', *Journal of the American Medical Association*, V256 (1986), p1768.

Bennett, F. J., 'AIDS as a social phenomenon', *Social Science and Medicine* V25 (1987) pp. 529–39.

Bove, J. R., R. Y. Dodd, W. V. Miller and S. G. Sandler 'How should we handle the ethical questions . . . in order to prevent transmission of AIDS by blood transfusion?', *Vox Sanguinis*, V49 (1985) pp. 234–9.

Boyd, K. M.,'The moral challenge of AIDS', *Journal of Royal Society of Medicine*, V80 (1987) pp. 281–3.

Cooke, M., 'Ethical issues in the care of patients with AIDS', *Quality Review Bulletin*, V12 (1986) pp. 343–6.

David, P.,'AIDS: moral majority intervenes', *Nature*, V304 (1983) p. 201.

Dilley, James W., E. E. Shelp and S. L. Batki 'Psychiatric and ethical issues in the care of patients with AIDS', *Psychosomatics*, V27 (1986) pp. 562–6.

Dominian, Jack, 'AIDS and morality',*The Tablet*, 10 Jan. 1987. p. 34.

Elford, J., 'Moral and social aspects of AIDS', *Social Science and Medicine*, V24 (1987) pp. 543–9.

'Ethical issues in psychological research on AIDS', *Journal of Homosexuality*, V13 (1986) pp. 109–16.

Faltz, B. G. and S. Madover, 'Treatment of substance abuse patients with HIV infection', *Advances in Alcohol and Substance Abuse*, V7 (1987) pp. 143–5.

Field, Martha A. and Kathleen M. Sullivan, 'AIDS and the criminal law', *Law, Medicine and Health Care*, V15 (1987) pp. 46–60.

Fineberg, Harvey V., 'Education to prevent AIDS: prospects and obstacles', *Science*, V239 (1988) pp. 592–6.

Fisher, Richard, 'AIDS and a plague mentality', *New Society*, 28 Feb. 1985, pp. 322–25.

'Frighten and be fired', *The Economist* 28 June 1986, pp. 39–40.

Gillett, Grant, 'AIDS and confidentiality', *Journal of Applied Philosophy*, V4 (1987) pp. 15–20.

Gillon, R., 'Testing for HIV Without Permission', *British Medical Journal*, V294 (1987) pp. 821–3.

Gillon, R., 'Refusal to treat AIDS and HIV-positive patients', *British Medical Journal*, V294 (1987) pp. 1332–3.

Gillon, R., 'AIDS and Medical Confidentiality', *British Medical Journal*, V294 (1987) pp. 1675–7.

Gostin, Larry, 'Draconian law or human decencies', *New Statesman*, 20 June 1986, pp. 17–18.

Gostin, Larry and William J. Curran, 'The limits of compulsion in controlling AIDS', *Hastings Center Report*, V16(6) Supp. (1986) pp. 24–9.

Gostin, L. and W. J. Curran, 'Legal control measures for AIDS', *American Journal of Public Health*, V77 (1987) pp. 214–18.

Gostin, L. and W. J. Curran, 'AIDS Screening, Confidentiality, and the

Duty to Warn', *American Journal of Public Health*, V77 (1987) pp. 361–5.

Gray, Lisbeth A. and Anna K. Harding, 'Confidentiality limits with patients who have the AIDS virus', *Journal of Counseling and Development*, V66 (1988) pp. 219–23.

Grodin, M. A., P. V. Kaminous and R. Sassower 'Ethical issues in AIDS research', *Quality Review Bulletin*, V12 (1986) pp. 347–52.

Gronfors, Martti and Olli Salstrom, 'Power, prestige, profit: AIDS and the oppression of homosexual people', *Acta Sociologica*, V30 (1987) pp. 53–66.

Habgood, John, 'By wayward values to new vulnerabilities', *The Times*, 13 Feb. 1987, p. 16.

Hayry, Heta and Matti Hayry, 'AIDS now', *Bioethics*, V1 (1987) pp. 339–56.

Hayry, Matti and Heta Hayry 'AIDS and a small north European country: a study in applied ethics', *International Journal Applied Philosophy*, V3 (1987) pp. 51–61.

Healy, C., 'AIDS and the professional ethic', *Australian Nurses Journal*, V14, p. 10, Feb. 1985.

Howe, E. G., 'Ethical aspects of military physicians treating patients with HIV', *Military Medicine*, V153 (1988) pp. 7–11; 72–6; 140–4.

Hume, Basil, 'AIDS – time for moral renaissance', *The Times*, 7 Jan. 1987, p. 10.

Johnson, Stephen D., 'Factors related to intolerance of AIDS victims', *Journal for the Scientific Study of Religion*, V26 (1987) pp. 105–10.

Judson, F. N. and T. M. Vernon 'The impact of AIDS on state and local health departments', *American Journal of Public Health*, V78 (1988) pp. 387–9.

Kain, Craig D., 'To breach or not to breach', *Journal of Counseling and Development*, V66 (1988) pp. 224–5.

Kayal, Philip M., 'Morals, medicine, and the AIDS epidemic', *Journal of Religion and Health*, V24 (1985) pp. 218–38.

Kirby, M. D., 'AIDS legislation – turning up the heat?', *Journal of Medical Ethics*, V12 (1986) pp. 187–94.

Levine, Carol, 'AIDS: an ethical challenge for our time', *Quality Review Bulletin*, V12 (1986) pp. 273–7.

Lumsden, Andrew, 'Desire and Mr Hayhoe', *New Statesman*, 29 Nov. 1985, pp. 14–15.

Macklin, R. and G. Friedland, 'AIDS research: the ethics of clinical trials', *Law, Medicine and Health Care*, V14 (1986) pp. 273–80.

Mariner, W. K. and R. C. Gallo, 'Getting to market: the scientific and legal climate for an AIDS vaccine', *Law, Medicine and Health Care*, V15 (1987) pp. 17–26.

Meisenbach, A. E., 'Reflections on the moral dimension of the AIDS epidemic', *Journal of American College Health*, V35 (1987) pp. 279–81.

Miles, Caroline, 'The battle against AIDS', *The Tablet*, 3 Jan. 1987, pp. 6–7.

Millan, G. and M. W. Ross, 'AIDS and gay youth', *Community Health Studies*, V11 (1987) pp. 50–3.

Miller, D., D. J. Jeffries, J. Green, J. R. W. Harris and A. J. Pinching 'HTLV-III: Should Testing ever be Routine?', *British Medical Journal*, V292 (1986) pp. 941–3.

Miller, W. V. and E. R. Simon, 'AIDS, ethics, and the blood supply', *Transfusion*, V25 (1985) pp. 174–5.

Mohr, Richard D., 'AIDS, gays, and state coercion', *Bioethics*, V1 (1987) pp. 35–50.

Mohr, R. D., 'Policy, ritual, purity: gays and mandatory AIDS testing', *Law, Medicine and Health Care*, V15 (1987) pp. 178–85.

'A moral and social crisis', *The Tablet*, 15 Nov. 1986, p. 1219.

Musto, David F., 'Quarantine and the problem of AIDS', *Milbank Quarterly*, V64, Supp. 1 (1986) pp. 97–117.

Neuberger, J., 'AIDS and the moral majority', *Nursing Times*, V82, 19 Nov. 1986, p. 22.

O'Neill, Sophie, 'AIDS: a women's concern', *Nursing Times*, V83, 7 Aug. 1988, p. 26.

O'Sullivan, John, 'Rights before responsibility', *The Times*, 12 Oct. 1985, p. 8.

Oppenheimer, Gerald M. and Robert A. Padgug, 'AIDS: the risk to insurers, the threat to equity', *Hastings Center Report*, V16(5) (1986) pp. 18–22.

Panem, S., 'AIDS, public policy, and biomedical research', *Chest*, V85 (1984) pp. 416–22.

Parent, B., 'Moral, ethical, and legal aspects of infection control', *American Journal of Infection Control*, V13 (1985) pp. 278–80.

Pascal, Chris B., 'Selected legal issues about AIDS for drug abuse treatment programmes', *Journal of Psychoactive Drugs*, V19 (1987) pp. 1–12.

Piorkowski, Joseph D., 'Between a rock and a hard place: AIDS and the conflicting physician's duties of preventing disease transmission and safeguarding confidentiality', *Georgetown Law Review*, V76 (1987) pp. 169–202.

Plumeri, P. A., 'The refusal to treat: abandonment and AIDS', *Journal of Clinical Gastroenterology*, V6 (1984) pp. 281–4.

Posey, E. Carol, 'Confidentiality in an AIDS support group', *Journal of Counseling and Development*, V66 (1988) pp. 226–7.

Prescott, James W., 'AIDS, sexual oppression and violence: a call for prevention', *The Humanist*, V47 Jul/Aug. 1987, pp. 15–17, 36.

Rabin, J. A., 'The AIDS epidemic and gay bathhouses: a constitutional analysis', *Journal of Health Politics, Policy and Law*, V10 (1986) pp. 729–47.

Radcliffe, Timothy, 'The church and AIDS' *The Tablet*, 8 Nov. 1986, p. 1210.

Remafedi, G. J., 'Preventing the sexual transmission of AIDS during adolescence', *Journal of Adolescent Health Care*, V9 (1988) pp. 139–43.

Silin, Jonathan G., 'The language of AIDS', *Teachers College Record*, V89 (1987) pp. 3–19.

Smith, R. J., 'Ethical decision-making: the principle of utility', *California Nurse*, V81(4) (1985) p. 6.

Smith, S. J., 'AIDS: ethical duties of nurses', *California Nurse*, V79(3) (1983) p. 4.

Stein, R. E., 'Avoiding conflict in AIDS cases', *Hastings Center Report*, V17(4) (1987) p. 4.

Steinbrook, R., B. Lo, J. Tirpack, J. W. Dilley and P. A. Volberding, 'Ethical dilemmas in caring for patients with the Acquired Immuno-deficiency Syndrome', *Annals of Internal Medicine*, V103 (1985) pp. 787–90.

'To let nurses work in ignorance is despicable, says College: nurses not told patients had AIDS', *Nursing Standard*, 17 Jan. 1985, p. 1.

Veitch, Andrew, 'AIDS extra: fighting bigotry as well as an epidemic', *Guardian*, 5 Nov. 1985, p. 11.

Velimirovic, B., 'AIDS as a social phenomenon', *Social Science and Medicine*, V25 (1987) pp. 541–52.

Vinogradov, Sophia, J. E. Thornton, A. J. Levinson and M. L. Callen 'Case study: "If I have AIDS, then let me die now" ', *Hastings Center Report*, V14(1) (1984) pp. 24–6.

Walter, L., 'Ethical issues in the prevention and treatment of HIV infection and AIDS', *Science*, V239 (1988) pp. 597–603.

Wiston, M. and S. H. Landesman 'AIDS and a duty to protect', *Hastings Center Report*, V17(1) (1987) pp. 22–3.

Young, E. W., 'AIDS: emerging moral questions', *Journal of American College Health*, V34(1986) pp. 240–2.

Name Index

176

Subject Index